NO CRY FOR HELP

NO CRY FOR HELP

RONALD H. MAYER

authorHOUSE®

AuthorHouse™
1663 Liberty Drive
Bloomington, IN 47403
www.authorhouse.com
Phone: 1-800-839-8640

Published by AuthorHouse   10/08/2012

ISBN: 978-1-4772-7100-1 (sc)
ISBN: 978-1-4772-7099-8 (e)

Library of Congress Control Number: 2012917147

PROLOGUE

This mystery begins with me, just a Marine wanting to go home to West Texas after eight hard years in the United States Marine Corps. I was a combat field staff officer with the rank of Captain and still only 27 years old, but I felt a hell of a lot older "with lots of years to give", so the Corps said.

I had been wounded in Vietnam toward the last of the so-called war, but I just hadn't been able to come back with a full stride. Accordingly the Corps gave me six months to get over it or get out.

My decision was to go back home where I had been raised as a kid on my grandfather's ranch near the little West Texas town of Spring Creek. Then maybe I would know just what I wanted to do with the rest of my life.

It All Started Right Here

On the way home I stopped off in Vegas for a little R&R, only to experience once again that I still didn't know how to shoot craps. Not surprisingly, I lost some of my hard earned savings on those pretty green tables.

Just as I was about to get my gear ready and head south, I stopped in at The Palace for one last look-see and maybe some newfound luck. With my last $50.00 of pocket money, I bought five $10.00 tickets on the Quick Pick Lottery and sat down to a fresh rum and coke and a look at the girls.

The giant screen began to announce the "get ready drawing" for the Quick Pick. The separate drawn numbers started appearing in a very fast order. I really wasn't overly interested in the drawing, until I took notice that my # I ticket, almost hidden in my little hot hand, was now showing four of the Quick Pick's winning numbers with number five just now being posted. It was a seven and I was now looking at the winning ticket, #24897, and thinking, "Whatever the prize is, it's mine."

The bells went off loudly and the screen began to flash. I turned cold and numb as I saw the dollar wheel kick in a special bonus prize for a total of FIVE MILLION DOLLARS. All I could think about was, "What a Homecoming!"

Now since you don't know me at all, I'm the quiet type. Because I don't like to draw too much attention, I just sat there preparing to breathe and steady myself, as I waited for all the hoop-la and confusion to settle back to what might be called normal in a place like this.

The Ring Master, as he is called, kept screaming out, "Is there a winner in this rowdy bunch? If so, step up and get famous. Why don't you buy the house a drink?"

That's just what I wasn't going to do, so I just sat tight and eventually got up and walked outside for some much needed fresh air.

Let me be the first to tell you. If you ever win some big money on a ticket raffle in Vegas, it's not anything easy like just walking up to the counter. presenting your winning ticket, quietly folding up your money and walking out, hoping no one is going to "big-deal" you or get next to you because you look lonely or something like that. If the Marine Corps had taught me anything, it was to recognize the enemy and always play it cool. "If you need to kill, shoot first and move on."

After about an hour, I walked into the Head Cashier's office and asked to see whoever was in charge of the Quick Pick Lottery. In about a second's time, this great looking blonde secretary perked up and said, "Do you have the winning ticket?"

I answered back as best I could, "I am that person."

Almost before I could ask what her name was, a door opened to the right of me, and the next voice I heard must have been that of the Head Cashier.

"Would you like to step into my office?"

So I did and to shorten this big payout event some, I spent the next several hours in what seemed to be too personal of a discussion about me, not to mention lots of paper signing and an unexpected visit from the duty IRS Agent.

Well, after Nevada tax and enough money to support Uncle Sam's needs for a few seconds, I ended up with something just over Three Million Three Hundred Ninety Eight Thousand Dollars. I took it in a certified cashier's check, folded up my copies of the great give-away and asked how I could exit this place unnoticed. That's what I wanted and had already signed off on being a Non-Recognized Statement Clause. I did not want any published notice of the fact I was the newest Quick Pick winner this great day in June of 1975.

I went out to the parking lot feeling as if I was being followed and headed for my 1970 model second hand Ford Sedan. Next stop, Bank of America where I deposited all but $20,000.00 hard cash in the name of Ron Heard, Spring Creek, Texas. At that time, my thoughts drifted back to the great looking blonde secretary and I sort of dreamt of another weekend in Vegas.

A Marine Training Signal, once absorbed and cataloged in my message center, was now flashing as an exposed vapor message, "The Enemy is always alert and can change the course of events, if you're careless." Remember, if you "need to kill, shoot first and move on."

I decided to head to West Texas. It was a nice drive past the Hoover Dam and on down to Flagstaff where I spent the night at The American Motel. You're right! I got the best damn room money could buy, ordered up a $22.50 New York Strip Steak and managed to put down two rum and cokes. It came to me all of a sudden, "I think I'm going to like being rich."

Next day, I drove southeast to Socorro, New Mexico, and on down to El Paso, Texas, where I spent another great night at The Marriott Hotel and decided not to go over to Mexico for a spin-through Juarez and an evening's fun. The old saying goes, "Let's not push your luck." Hell, I'm batting way over 1000 now.

The next day, as I headed east toward Spring Creek, a kind of funny feeling kept pushing its way forward into my fractional being. This feeling of another presence in or around me is not a new feeling. I've always known I am sort of like two different people who share the same moment but with different understandings and intentions. This interference to my present thinking comes on without invitation and almost always is a forceful intrusion into my thought patterns.

One person, being the "proper me," is a determined, disciplined and trustworthy Red Blooded American. You know, the type you might want to take home to meet your folks, while the other uninvited person or feeling is a chance taker, somewhat ornery or sometimes just plain evil and can be wicked, most always capable of pushing you to the limit of your once good intentions.

So now you know how things come and go as to my thought process and to whatever intentions, good or bad. The question now before me or should I say, us, was, "What the hell am I going to do with all this money? I didn't earn it, and God knows I don't deserve it."

The Second Marine, the other me, which I will refer to as M#2, came up with a funny little laugh and stated, "Just whose business is it that you have so damn much money? So, don't let's get stupid and say we don't deserve it. After all, it was our money we spent on that hotshot ticket and it proved we were right on. And besides, it was way past our time for a little luck. Have you already forgotten we've been to hell and back these last eight years?"

I was quick to try to focus on the better side of the interruption of the moment and push back the mean streak that always seemed to follow these uninvited intentions.

Hell, all of a sudden it came to me, "I'm going to buy me a cattle ranch of my very own and live the good old rancher life from here on out. I don't have to take orders from no one. I'll give no quarter to anyone ever again."

M#2 came right back and said, "Have you gone plumb stupid? You're talking about work! You know, sweaty, dirty clothes, poor eats and long hours just to prove you can be a real cowboy. You must be coming unglued. I thought we finished up with that lifestyle back in the Good Old U.S. Marines."

Nevertheless, I'm running this show and I said, "I'm going to buy me a West Texas Cattle Ranch, like it or not. If you're not with me, you're against me. You make the call."

It appeared M#2 was more than ever so quick and ready with his sarcastic remarks and I was getting damn tired of it. So I devised a means to rid myself of this instant and constant interruption from my subconscious. I simply pushed my lips together and with a quick rush of air from way down inside the emotions of my soul, I made this sound that sounded like "whiff", or maybe like you're spitting and no spit comes out. At any rate, that was the new way I could get M#2 out of sight and out of mind for that moment.

LET'S TALK RANCHES

I arrived in Spring Creek just before noon and it appeared things were much the same as I remembered they were so many years back. So I just ambled over to the cafe to see what the lunch special was for this Tuesday, June 3, 1975. After lunch I just drifted on over to the bank to see if they knew if there were any good West Texas Ranches for sale in these parts.

Right off, I recognized old man G.S. McGinnis, who by this time must have owned the whole damn bank, because when I was in this very bank with my grandfather so many years ago, old man G.S. McGinnis was always sitting right where he is today. Granted he's now much older, but so am I. So I gave him a chance to look me over, as he and everyone in the bank were doing at this time. I guess they had never seen a Marine Captain up this close.

At last he gave up on the looking and came right out and said, "Ain't you one of them Heard boys from over to the Middle Concho Ranch?"

"Yes, Sir," I said, "That's me. Could I have just a little of your time about a matter that needs to be discussed with an expert?"

"Damn right, boy, just what seems to be bothering you this fine day?" the old man belted out.

I went over the fact that I was just back from the Vietnam War and wanted to settle on a nice little cattle ranch in this part of West Texas and the best part of this request was that I thought I could afford to make a purchase, providing I like the ranch.

Old man G.S. just reared back and began to laugh and almost got choked down, until he coughed a few times, Then he came right out and said, "Boy, do you have any idea about how much hard money it takes to buy some of this here land?"

All of a sudden M#2 took over and said, "Listen, you old SOB, you can call me Captain, you can call me Marine or even by my given name, Ron, but hear this, don't ever call me, BOY!"

I guess this sudden out-burst from what appeared to be me was sufficient enough to make the old man come to a better opinion of just who he was talking to, because he said, "OK, Ron. I do know of a nice ranch that's going to be auctioned off this Saturday at 10 o'clock right on the front steps of the Irion County Courthouse. But, Marine, you need to know right up front, it could bring as much as $1,500,000.00 or more and I'm sure there are going to be some big spenders here opening and shutting down the bids with good old West Texas oil money drippings."

He then went on to name the ranch as the old Tom Tyler Ranch just 10 miles south of town on the El Dorado Road. Seems poor Tom had just ranched himself out of money and couldn't pay his way any more, so Mr. G.S. McGinnis and the other bank board folks just called his note and I bet for damn sure they pushed to be first on the list to get paid.

I told Mr. G.S. that I had some money saved in a bank in Nevada and asked him what was the best way to get some of those funds transferred down to his nice little bank here in Spring Creek. Old man G.S. called over to his assistant and the process of transferring Two Million Dollars from one bank to another took place without a word, other than the entire bank staff of about six people all had their eyes on just who the hell was this Marine with a deposit of $2,000,000.00 who just walked into the Spring Creek Independent Bank.

Dove Creek Ranch

The brochure I ended up with gave the details on the ranch. Its acreage was almost 11,000 deeded acres, seven fenced pastures, five windmills with storage tanks and cattle drinkers. The entire ranch was fenced and crossed fenced with net wire and four strands of barbwire. Then there was a complete display of pictures of the headquarters and some good pictures of the ranch pastures and the live water, Dove Creek, that passes through the north part of the ranch in the #4 pasture. At the end of the brochure was a directive about the ranch tour to take place on Friday, the day before the auction. And in quotations, the flyer said, "No livestock goes with the sale of this property."

M#2 pops up with, "I guess we better change our clothes and try to look more like the natives, if we are going to try to fit in a little better with all these country bumpkins."

I simply refused to buy any brand of new cowboy clothes, such as Levis, a pearl button shirt and some shiny new boots. I guess I just wasn't ready to look brand new at this big juncture in my new found life.

That night at the motel I just dug through my duffle bag and found a set of old khakis and my field combat boots. I took all the insignias off the shirt and, all of a sudden, I looked sort of normal for the first time in a long time.

I showed up at the Tyler Ranch at the proper time for the tour and was met by of group of 15 or so. I guess you would call them ranch buyers, because they came to see the Tom Taylor Ranch, or maybe they just came to eat the Bar-B-Q. I could have saved all these folks a lot of heartache and trouble, because I was going to own this very ranch by this time tomorrow. The ranch tour was great, lots of things to look at and try to digest in such a short time.

The main house was located in a big grove of oak trees and was constructed of native rock with big front windows and a once beautiful back yard patio, now grown up in weeds and in need of lots of repair to get it back to its original attractive condition. In fact, the main house, bunkhouse and barn could all use a complete overhaul. It appeared that all the improvements had been neglected for several years. All it would take was time and money, so it was no big deal to me. It seemed that I had plenty of both.

Fact was, the entire ranch was run down and in need of much repair and a little TLC. If I could get it bought, I would someday need to think about what kind of cattle and horses I needed to complete this wild ass dream that M#2 was having so much trouble living with.

THE AUCTION DAY

I had been staying in a motel in Angelo, just 40 miles east of Spring Creek. It was a delightful drive into Spring Creek each day and especially today, The Big Auction Day of the Old Tom Tyler Ranch.

This Saturday morning early, before heading out to Spring Creek, I drove out to the Stockyards Cafe for a good, greasy West Texas Breakfast. This was the same old cafe my grandfather liked to eat at years ago and sometimes I had been lucky enough to get an invitation to come along, as long as I didn't talk too much to all his cowboy friends.

As I remembered, I sure did enjoy my early life with my grandfather and all the things he let me do with him. If you didn't have a grandfather like mine, you've sure as hell missed out on a lot of things that are fun to just sit and think about.

As I entered the café, I noticed most everything was just how I wanted to remember it was so many years ago. I sat down next to a bunch of old cowboy type men and ordered up a cup of good strong coffee. I sort of felt like I needed it, because this was the day I was going to buy my first West Texas Ranch, "Come Hell or High Water!"

As I was just sitting there minding my own business, one of the old cowboys turned to me and said, "Ain't you that same fellow I seen at the Old Tom Tyler Ranch yestiddy? Just who might you be?" He went on to say, "My name is Tom J. Foster, but most everyone around here calls me, Tommy. So what did you say your name was?"

"I didn't say, but since you're so damn pushy, I go by the name of Ron Heard."

He jumped right back at me and said, "Is you one of them Heard boys from over to the Middle Concho Ranch?"

"Yes, I was, or I am, but I don't think you know me. I was just a kid some 16 years or so ago when I used to spend time on the ranch with my grandfather."

"Hell, yes, I remember," Tommy blurts out, "You was that little kid that was always talking and asking us cowboy questions."

About that time all the other old men sitting at the table with Tommy began to take a better look at me from top to bottom. Tommy continued talking, as if I needed to hear all the remarks about my upbringing on the Middle Concho Ranch.

Finally one of the other men said, "Give it a rest, Tommy. Maybe this fellow don't care nothing about you rattling on about his past."

My food showed up and so I just turned into myself and started eating a great West Texas Breakfast. Tommy turned around once again and delivered me one hell of a message that caused me to take a deep look at Tom J. Foster.

He said, "I was the cow foreman for old man Tom Tyler on that there same ranch I saw you at just yestiddy. Yeah, I damn sure was for 10 years and I know where every damn slick rock is on that ranch and a hell of lot more. So Mr. Middle Concho Ranch fellow, if you get that SOB bought, you just come looking for Tom J. Foster, 'cause I can still make a day's wages and I will do my level best to change you into the cowboy your grandfather trained you to be."

M#2 jumped right in and informed me that it looks like I was going to be the head housekeeper for all the old wornout cowboys in all of West Texas and no doubt we could look forward to getting some of the same treatment in the years to come, since the dye is cast for all us Middle Concho Cowboys. I came up with a strong "whiff' and M#2 hurried to get out of the way.

I took the nice slow drive out to Spring Creek with great expectations on the upcoming day's event. I had not changed my mind. I still wanted to own the Tom Tyler Ranch, so M#2 did his best to keep his thoughts in my mind. I said, "Let's get onto the 'goat roping'." That's cowboy talk for, "Look sharp, the main event is coming up sooner than you think."

It's Time . . . The Main Event

The Courthouse parking lot was already filling up with lots of cars, but mostly pickups, and the crowd was made up of mostly straw hats and Levis with dirty, dusty boots.

However, there were a few city types all hanging in one well polished group. You know the type; low quarter shoes, shiny trousers and a nice, clean, freshly laundered white shirt. I could tell they were "Oilies", because they all seemed to be wearing The Nose Picker Style $10,000 Rolex Watch. You know, the one with the big solid gold band. Yeah, you got to look at it every time one of them Oilies picked at his nose. I felt like I could almost see their checkbooks bulging out of their shirt pockets.

M#2 says, "Hold on, fellows, we Middle Concho Boys don't go bear hunting with a switch."

I walked up to the Special Master's table and noticed old man G.S. McGinnis was kind of holding court with a bunch of would-be buyers who had just qualified to be a bidder. All of a sudden, he spotted me and hollered out, "Hey, Ron, come on over here and sign up and get your number for the auction. I think we are just about to get this show under way. Did you bring your checkbook?"

M#2 says, "Damn sure we did, old man. Do you think we came all the way from California to just say, 'Howdy, Boys'?" I drew Number 12, which meant there were 11 bidders ahead of me and a few more were already standing at the table to be given a number. It was beginning to look like no one present was going to steal this ranch, that is, if I could help it from happening.

THE TIME IS NOW

The Special Master for this bankrupt ranch sale was old Charlie Jennings. He was, and I think had always been, one of the four County Commissioners for Irion County. Seemed I remembered his name from a long way's back. He now stood up and read off the proclamation about why the ranch was being auctioned off on Saturday, the 7th of June 1975, right here on the Courthouse steps of Spring Creek, Texas, and that all the creditors would be paid first in line from the proceeds of the sale of The Tom Tyler Ranch.

He went on to say that the opening bid of $85.00 a deeded acre would include any mineral acres The Tyler Ranch owned, if there were any, and the opening bid had been set by His Honor, Judge Fred Shultz, the District Judge for Irion County, Texas. Just as quick as you could say "you all", someone hollered out, "I give $90.00 hard cash" and the crowd woke up to the big event.

All of a sudden we were talking about money and at this point we were already just a little shy of a One Million Dollar Bid, and I hadn't even had a chance to bid. M#2 said, "Get with it, Captain, or we are going to be back in the Good Old U.S. Marine Corps, where we ought to be anyway."

"BS," I whispered and raised my sign stating #12, "I bid $95.00 dollars a deeded acre, same kind of money, hard cash."

M#2 said, "Damn you, Spring Creek People. We've done spent our first Million Dollars and it looks like we don't even own the ranch."

Just then a new bid of $100.00 a deeded acre hit the crowd like a hammer. I just stood there a minute to see who was bidding against who when the new standing bid of $100.00 a deeded acre went to $105.00 and started to hover just a little. However, it wasn't for long, because I up and bid $110.00 a deeded acre without any hesitation. I hoped everyone saw my firmness and conviction. So much for my ego!

With new disappointment, some Oilie just up front from me made a big issue of the fact that he could bid $115.00 a deeded acre, and so he did. The rest of the bidders seemed to have had all they needed and were sort of just looking on to see who the biggest spender was going to be. The bid was $1,265,000.00 and was kind of holding in limbo, with the Special Master calling out, "Is there anyone else who wants to top this $115.00 a deeded acre offering?"

M#2 says, "Damn right, we do," and I came up with an unrehearsed bid of $122.50 a deeded acre. That bid stopped the chatter and directed everyone's attention over toward me to see just who in the hell was this Plain Jane type of person bidding all this money.

The Special Master again was trying to work the crowd for just one more bid, but there didn't seem to be anymore players, until an offer of $125.00 a deeded acre was coughed up by another one of them Oilies. I countered this poor attempt to cut me out of the bidding and upped the bid to $130.00 a deeded acre. M#2 reminded me that our last bid was close to $1,500,000.00, which he thought was going to be my limit, if push came to shove.

No action was forthcoming from any place in the crowd, so the Special Master was forced to start the final phase of the bidding with a loud, "We have one hundred thirty dollars a deeded acre bid. Going once, going twice," and he held up for what seemed a long stretch and then capped it off with, "Going three times and THE RANCH IS SOLD TO THE DISTINGUISHED LOOKING YOUNG MAN IN THE KHAKI CLOTHES. What is your name, Number 12? Will it be cash or check?"

Mr. G.S. McGinnis spoke up and said that he'd give a draft for the full amount on the Spring Creek Independent Bank of Irion County, Texas.

I was feeling a little jumpy, having done such a thing, but I sure knew I had done the right thing and if M#2 was going to experience any "Buyer's Remorse", to go on and get over it, because from here on out, my home was going to be on the Old Tom Tyler Ranch, which I will now call Dove Creek Ranch. I went over to the Courthouse and signed all the papers and asked them to record everything in the name of the ranch, Dove Creek Ranch, Ron Heard, Owner.

This Is As Good As It Gets

I fooled around Spring Creek the rest of the afternoon, just getting acquainted with the town and the people who made this little trade center a great little West Texas town and a nice place to live. I met a lot of nice folks and sure got some good advice on how to manage the Old Tom Tyler Ranch and already some requests for me to let people come fishing on Dove Creek.

I headed for Angelo to get the rest of my gear and close out the motel I had been staying at. All of a sudden, I remembered my last conversation with Tom J. Foster, the old cowboy who wanted to go to work for me, if I up and bought the Tyler Ranch, the same ranch he had worked on for so many years.

The next morning, I headed for the cafe and sure enough right out front just this side of the front door was a bed roll, an old saddle and a few of his things tied up in a cardboard box. As I entered the cafe, I noticed the same bunch of old cowboys sitting at their personal table drinking coffee and, for sure, Tommy was right there, expecting me to show up.

He hollered out, "Hey, Boss, I got my entire gear ready and I'm ready to 'walk a mile,' so let's go do some work on our new ranch."

I sat down and had a cup of coffee and sure enough got some more advice on how to run a West Texas Ranch. I signaled Tommy to let's get this show on the way and make tracks for the ranch or "walk a mile," whatever that means.

As we headed out of town for the ranch, the three of us seemed rather quiet and more or less pleased with what had come to pass, regarding the purchasing of the ranch and all the things that lay ahead of us. M#2 was quiet to a point and got a little restless, as Tommy began to talk about all the work that needed to be done to bring the ranch up to par. He mentioned working on all the fences and, for sure, bringing all the windmills up online and seeing that they were pumping the right amount of water.

Then he asked me right out, "What are we going to do about the headquarters ranch house and the bunkhouse? Seems they were sure run down and would need a major overhauling and major clean-up outside and inside, if we are to ever enjoy living out here in the country."

I said, "I am going to hire it out to people who know how to do this kind of work. I don't do windows and neither does M#2."

The next day Old Cowboy Tommy went into El Dorado and got a herd of Dry and Wet Mexicans and by sunset, things were sure looking much better around Dove Creek Ranch. The crew went to work on the bunkhouse first and scraped and scrubbed the entire wood frame house both inside and outside.

I remembered as a young boy over to the Middle Concho Ranch headquarters that my grandmother used to pour extra strength Clorox over all the bathrooms and kitchen floors once a month to keep things nice and clean for her family, who never really appreciated the many things she did to keep our ranch running up to par.

I headed into El Dorado to buy enough Clorox to get both the bunkhouse and the big house free from bugs, spiders and rattlesnakes or whatever else had taken up residence in these houses since old Tom Tyler up and shut things down almost a year ago.

After the big pour, Tommy moved right into the bunkhouse and spread out his bedroll on the floor and never seemed to give a notice to the strong smell of Clorox that was still trying to dry out. I myself just couldn't stand it, so M#2 and I just slept in the old car until we could get up enough nerve to try the big house.

IT's MY CALL

Next day or so Tommy came right out and said, "Boss Man, we need to get this here ranch a pickup truck of some kind so we can get around the ranch to check on what's going on in and around this property."

So off we all went in the old Ford Sedan, headed again to El Dorado to see who had the best deal on pickups. We took a vote going into town and it was decided that all three of us would give a description of the pickup he thought might be the best for the ranch and, for sure, the cowboys. Tommy said we needed a Dodge, because they are tough and can stand lots of hard work. M#2 suggested we buy a Chevy, because his grandfather used to have one when he was a kid working on the family ranch. I said I think Fords are the best ranch pickups for this area of West Texas and I based that on the clear fact that this very morning as we drove by the Post Oak Cafe here in El Dorado, there were nine Ford pickups compared to two Chevys and no Dodge pickups at the cafe this day.

At that, I turned into the Ford Garage right here on Main Street in El Dorado. Got next to nothing for the old Ford Sedan as a trade-in and paid hard cash money for a nice, white 150 Ford, four wheel drive, loaded with all the bells and whistles. Needless to say, we were a proud bunch, as we headed to the ranch after buying a full pickup load of groceries.

It's Not Work, If You Enjoy It

The Mexican boys under Tommy's direction were cleaning as best they could or knew how to. Then Tommy would make them do it over again, just to make sure nothing was left out. I counted five one-gallon empty Clorox containers on the front porch of the Big House, so I guessed everything was almost clean when M#2 and I moved in to sleep on the floor.

Earlier I had gotten the working crew to take all the furniture out back to get a better look at it and to decide if I wanted to clean it up and continue to use it. I had hoped it would freshen up and quit smelling so rank after a day or two in the hot sun. Come to find out, it just wasn't going to air out.

Maybe the next trip to El Dorado we could find someone to come out and replace all the appliances. I guessed we would just buy a pickup load of furniture or maybe start with at least one bed. Hell, M#2 could just sleep on the clean floor, for all I cared.

The Mexican crew that Tommy hired did most of the pasture fence repairs. When the needed repair work was finished, all the Wets had vamoosed, that is to say, they had been paid and left Dove Creek Ranch for work elsewhere. These Mexican boys had been good help and the fact of the matter was they were the only help we could get to do this kind of manual labor. I felt good about the way I treated them, even if it went against the grain, as far as M#2 was concerned. You see, M#2 gives no quarter to aliens from any country.

If you come in the back way to the ranch from Spring Creek, you have to turn off the main paved road west to El Dorado, just four miles out of town and then proceed on County Road CC 26 for about six miles, until you come to what is called, "The Junction."

You will know you're at this spot because the road comes to a dead stop and you then need to turn left to go the next six miles on into El Dorado. Just across from the Junction Stop on your right is a large stand of four, big live oak trees, partly on the road right of way and the other two just across the fence, which by the way is on my Dove Creek side.

Straight on down this same road 1.5 miles or so is the main gate to the ranch. You can easily see the entrance, because I still haven't taken down the old Tom Tyler ranch sign. At The Junction location and next to the two live oak trees, the County has placed a trash bin or dumpster for trash collection, because all the kids from around these parts seemed to have renamed this particular spot, "Lovers' Hide Out", or just a good place to hide out and drink beer and maybe smoke a little pot.

Therefore, once a week or so the road crew comes by to clean up the trash and bottles and haul off the full dumpster, replacing it with an empty one. I got to where I liked to come from town this way, mainly because you get to see the countryside. I always give a little thanks when I begin to pass right in front of my very own West Texas Ranch.

Last time I came by the Hide Out, I noticed that someone had cut a good size hole in my pasture fence, right behind the trees and there were lots of tracks going and coming into my #2 pasture. I made a note to come up from the house through the #1 pasture and repair this fence. No doubt I need to check and see what the hell is taking place on my property.

THE MAIN EVENT

I was about six weeks into being a brand new ranch owner and enjoying every damn minute of it, even if M#2 did nothing but complain about the work, the food and the fact we didn't have any furniture yet in the big house.

After we completed washing and scrubbing the inside of the big house, I decided to get rid of all the appliances and furniture and just buy everything new. I believe it's called a "turn key deal" and will make the inside of the house over to be just what I want, even if I don't know what I want, or how to get it done. I gave everything in the house, which was old and musty smelling, to a needy family from El Dorado for extra clean up work to be done in and around the house whenever I called them to come out and help me out.

About the time things got to going pretty good, Tommy took sick and I had to take him back to town. I made sure the lady at the boarding house took good care of him and I left her with enough money to do this chore and a note telling her how I could be reached if Tommy needed anything. Tommy had been a great companion and had done everything I needed, which made it a lot easier, due to the many years he had been doing this kind of ranch work and right on this very ranch.

I now almost knew where every slick rock on The Dove Creek Ranch was located. I would miss the old cowboy and I bet a nickel M#2 felt the same. I sure hoped that he would get up and going and would give me a call.

NO CRY FOR HELP

Today, Saturday the 14th of July, 1975, I had been away from the United States Marine Corps for almost two wonderful months.

I don't believe I had even missed it one bit, even though M#2 kept reminding me I was up for promotion to Major and all I had to do was call Headquarters and tell them I was doing great and would be coming back to duty at the end of my recuperation period. I guess I hadn't made it clear to M#2 yet, but "that dog just don't hunt." I liked the new cowboy rancher life that had come to me on a silver platter. Therefore I felt like it was going to be "goodbye to Good Old Uncle Sam and the United States Marine Corps."

This Saturday, even though it looked like it might rain, I decided to get over to the #2 pasture and fix the fence that the kids had cut the big hole in and see just what was so interesting down in the bushes behind the trees. I drove the pickup through #1 and crossed into #2 and headed as best I could for "The Hide Out" to make the repairs needed to the fence.

The ranch road I was traveling on began to peter out about a quarter mile from where I thought the location might be, so I got out and started walking, carrying two cedar posts, some baling wire, and fence pliers. You couldn't see too far ahead of you, because the mesquite brush and the white brush had grown so thick in the bottoms you almost needed to get down on your hands and knees to get through the tangle of trees and brush.

I was beginning to wish I had gone on out the main gate and down the road to The Junction to do the fence repair work. When almost there, I first noticed it had started to sprinkle just a little. Then all of a sudden somewhere out ahead of me, I thought I heard some loud talking or maybe it was even some yelling. I stopped and tried to get my bearings and focus on what and where these strange voices were coming from. I edged my way forward through the brush entanglement. By this time, my Marine training was starting to click in and I was almost crawling toward the voices. M#2 clearly classified these strange sounds as, "The Enemy."

I crawled up to what appeared to be a small clearing and at this point my forward vision was straight to the right of the two big oak trees on the country right-of-way, just over my fence. There was a shiny, red, two door sedan parked just in front of the dumpster and both front doors were wide open and you could clearly see and hear two people yelling at each other, while they were sort of wrestling in the front seat of the car.

I heard a woman's voice forcibly say, "You SOB, get the hell off me. Just what the hell do you think doing?"

The yelling quickly turned into screaming and again I clearly heard her scream, "Get the hell off me."

Now I heard a man's voice in a very gruff, forceful tone say, "Go to hell, you blonde bitch. You set me up for this and now I want what you been teasing me with for the last hour."

At that very moment I heard the woman painfully scream out and at the same time, a heavy thud sound to what must have been a blow to her body or maybe even her face. I couldn't see all the happenings due to my low position in the brush, but I figured the man was going to forcefully rape her, even if he had to beat the hell out of her in the process.

I moved a little to the right and could see one of her legs was up over the front seat, indicating the attacker had already forced her over on her back. The moaning and screaming kept coming along with some choice words from the assailant, as he continued to assault the victim physically with a clear intent and purpose in what he was about to do.

Both M#2 and I almost automatically at the same time made our way through the brush and were just about over the fence when our recognizance mission was halted by the sudden piercing sound of a pistol shot that caused this Marine to hit the dirt, so to speak, and roll back further into the brush for better cover. After hitting the ground, I rolled over on my left side to keep the car in sight.

Both front doors were still opened full and I could see both bodies still entangled, the attacker still on top of the victim. The only noise coming from the car was that of the woman who was still screaming and moaning and apparently doing her best to get free of this forced-on position of a grown man lying on top of her. I continued to hold my position and view the action scene.

Almost immediately, after struggling to get free and now with great effort, the woman had managed to turn completely over on her stomach, face down in the seat. She was now doing her best to rise up on her hands and knees. It seemed clear from this point that the woman was the shooter, because the attacker was now quiet and limp and showed no resistance to her frantic movements.

About this time, I noticed the sudden appearance of a great amount of blood not only on the clothing of the woman and the man, but it was now smeared all over the front seat, starting to run off the seat onto the surface of the ground just outside the open door. The woman who was still screaming and cussing but now had somehow managed to rise up onto her hands and knees to a position and height that caused the attacker's body to slide forward in a very limp form.

With one last heaving effort from the woman, his entire body pitched, rolled forward and slowly somersaulted over and out of the front seat, landing face up on his back on the ground next to the driver side of the car. The woman now began to slide her body, feet first, pushing with her hands and sliding on her stomach through the pool of blood on the seat. Her body was pushed out of the front seat of the car onto the passenger side and through the still open door.

At this very moment, M#2 rose up and started for the fence. I don't know what he had in mind, but I sure didn't like this sudden unplanned move, for whatever reason. I quickly suggested we give this action scene some more time, due mainly to fact that the woman was still holding a revolver in her left hand. Even though she appeared to be badly beaten and dazed, along with being covered in fresh red blood, she could still be very dangerous. In fact her classification had now changed from the victim to the attacker, since her one-time lover was bleeding out the rest of his life right here on County Road CC 26 in a West Texas rainstorm on this somewhat strange day in July of 1975.

The Intent Is Now Clear

The rain was starting to get heavier and now a slight west wind had begun to blow in. All of a sudden, the once clear-cut view of the action field faded, but I only had a foggy front view of the woman. Now she was standing on the outside of the car, facing my direction with the revolver still in her left hand.

Her appearance was shocking, if not pitiful, because more than likely just a short time ago and prior to this unexpected event, this woman had apparently been a very handsome female, I'd say between 25 and 30 years old, standing about 5ft. 4 inches and weighing in at around 110 pounds or so. She wore her hair short and it was something like a sand shade of blonde. Her clothes, what was left of them, were sporty; a khaki skirt and what was left of a white blouse.

The attacker had worked her over in a very rough manner, while trying to gain a position in reference to what he was after. He had torn the front out of her blouse and partly torn her bra in half exposing her right breast. Her left eye was swollen almost shut and she was bleeding from a large cut several inches up into her hair line above her left eyebrow. No doubt she had taken a powerful physical beating from this one-time lover in just the few minutes that I observed the struggle. Now the rain was coming down in sheets and she was being washed of most of the blood that had already stained her clothing and front profile from head to toe. She was getting a free wash job from the rain, but I felt sure she hadn't given the weather much thought at this point.

Each step she took was an effort, due to the sudden accumulation of mud forming in the low spot where she had parked the car just a short time ago. With the mud rapidly mixing with the bloody water and gathering in small pools created by her footprints, this woman was no doubt terribly stressed out. I doubt if she knew where she was or how she got here.

The victim had started moving toward the rear of the car, holding on, as she worked her way through the rain and mud, evidently going over to check on her one time lover.

M#2 observed, "That guy is dead for sure; you can't lose that much blood and still have rape on your mind."

As she staggered forward through the rain, her next two turns put her right in front of the now downed man she had just shot.

"No doubt it was self defense," M#2 continued.

I started once again to climb over the fence to see if I could help this poor woman who was in such distress. After all, I was a witness to what I thought her claim of self-defense would be based on. M#2 was uncomfortable with this sudden move on my part and reminded me that she was still holding the revolver in her left hand and it appeared that she knew how to use it.

Before I could come up with an argument about how I'd charmed a lot of women for one thing or another, two quick shots rang out on the driver's side of the sedan. No chance for my intervention now and thanks to M#2 for that expression of caution because this Blonde Bitch, as she was now being called, would require a change in her defense plea from self defense to murder.

DEADLY IS THE BLACK WIDOW

M#2 had now given her the title of, "The Dove Creek Black Widow," because her scenario these past few minutes was very similar to the dance of the Female Black Widow Spider when she's in heat and needs to entice her suitor to mate in her nest. If he doesn't measure up, she kills him and then wraps him up and gets rid of him. I think she gets rid of him, even if he did do what he was destined to do.

At any rate, the once seemingly charming young woman was now standing over the man she had just shot three times, screaming, crying and cussing either about this West Texas rainstorm or the turn of events that have now entered her world with such violence. She now made a sudden turn toward where I was lying and it appeared she was looking right at me. However, my cover was good, due to the clothes I was wearing and the thickness of the brush all around me.

As I lay there, motionless, in the wet grass and patches of mud, wondering just what to do next, she screamed out, "What have I done to deserve this kind of treatment?" The rain was still falling in sheets and for a moment I'd again lost sight of the Black Widow, but I could hear some very heavy distinct and different sounds around where I last saw her standing.

M#2 continued to disagree with my lay-low position; it seemed he now wanted to force some sort of action on our part or, could it be, on her part.

As the storm began to clear a little, I saw her back for a moment. She bent forward, as if she was pulling, or should I say, struggling to drag something out away from the car. Damn if I didn't believe the Black Widow was now trying to drag the body of her now dead lover to the dumpster next to one of the trees, for what other reason than to be disposed of and hauled away someday, along with the other trash.

M#2 chimed in at this point, "If she can get that limp man's body in that dumpster under these conditions, I don't think we want any part of her."

The struggle continued until she had the body partly leaning up against the dumpster, resting more or less facing forward. By this time, the once victim, now the perpetrator, was covered in mud with red blood-stained clothing, still bleeding from the deep cut in her hairline. She was standing facing the car with her back to me and the dumpster, when just that fast she dropped down out of my sight. No doubt on her knees, she was again struggling with the body, all the time still moaning and cussing this rainy West Texas day or several other things that might have gone wrong for her this Saturday, July 14, 1975.

Almost as fast as she disappeared, she again resurfaced; however, this time she had somehow gotten down on all fours and forced her head through the mud in order to get her head and shoulders up and between the dead man's legs and into the crotch area of the unfortunate bygone lover. With unprecedented determination she was now starting to heave, push and lift the body toward the open lid of the dumpster, the entire body weight on her neck and shoulders under almost impossible conditions.

I had now moved my position somewhat forward to get a better view of this unbelievable Irion Woman Event that was unfolding right here in front of me. Right about now, she seemed to have the body pulled and lifted about halfway up the face side of the open dumpster, still struggling as she was slipping backward in the mud.

With the same determination as the Black Widow Spider, wrapping up her now-dead male suitor, this Blonde Bitch was determined to rid herself of her onetime suitor. In this case, that meant dumping his now worthless carcass in the Irion County landfill, via the Junction Dumpster.

In one last great effort and with her body leverage, she now struggled to push and heave the limp body up, over, and into the dumpster. The surely dead one-time lover landed in a heap on top of the trash and whatever else the dumpster was hiding.

Again she turned toward where I was still lying, completely spent and holding on to the dumpster for support. The Black Widow looked as if she had just lost something and might need to look in the dumpster to find whatever she was searching for.

M#2 informed me that with the revolver now laying on the trunk of the car, this could be the right time to make our move and see what could be in this event for us. I had to whiff him off again, because I couldn't see that there was anything but trouble on the other side of this fence.

THE GET-A-WAY

The rain had started coming down again in sheets and not only was the Dove Creek Black Widow getting soaked, but this wannabe cowboy was plumb wet to his toenails and for sure there was no place to hide or go to get out of this storm until the events happening right in front of me settled back to some form of normal. This for sure was about the time M#2 got grumpier and started to lecture me on his favorite principle of, "Just what the hell are you going to do now?"

I suggested we wait on the shooter to make up her mind and then we decide what could be done to safeguard our rights. That is, if we have any left, after watching this murder take place. The lady in question was now no doubt struggling to deal with this horrible event that was before her at The Junction, a place that at one time offered her a much better time and satisfaction with her lover than the surprise she got today.

Still stressed out mentally and, for sure, physically, in a dark side condition that she had never had to deal with, she started to stagger away from her hold on the dumpster and more or less fell or slipped her way to the driver's side of the car. The door was still open and she managed to get in. For a moment, she put her still bleeding head on her arms that were holding onto the steering wheel.

The crying and screaming was ear piercing, even though the storm was still raging all around us and was getting more difficult to deal with. Now at last she seemed to have a little more control, so she shut her driver side door and attempted to slide across the front seat to reach out and close the passenger side door. This was proving to be more of a job than she counted on.

The front seat was still very slippery with the blood of her once sought after lover; you know, the one she had just hidden in the county dumpster for a free burial at the

Irion County landfill. She slipped and slid across the seat on her right side until she got hold of the far door and managed to slam it shut. Wet, bloody, tired and still in a state of hysteria, she started the Red Sedan.

M#2 and I had moved our position now even closer to see better, since the rain seemed to be tapering off once again.

The Dove Creek Black Widow was still just sitting in the car, no doubt with the heater running. Things might be getting a little clearer to the distressed driver who was wondering just what to do now.

Without warning the Red Sedan started up and splashed and spun out away from the dumpster, shooting mud off its back tires almost as far out as our hidden position.

M#2, without any care, obediently headed for the fence. Once over, he was at the dumpster, beginning to go through the personal effects of just who this guy was. "Let's just take a look to see what he has on his very dead person."

I was against this sort of dead man stripping, having had some experience with the troops when we wiped out the different enemy holdings in Vietnam. For some unknown reason, I seemed to be involved in what was taking place right before me in this very wet public dumpster.

As I looked down in the mud, I located the killer's tiny footprints. Not too far from where the car was parked was one of her low quarter slipper type shoes. It must have pulled off in the mud during her effort to bury Ted Long, her lost lover; at least, that was the name the dead man's wallet produced as to his identification.

Death At High Speed

We had now collected, or should I say" stolen," Ted's wallet and a fancy Rolex watch, and a 1967 Texas A&M Class Ring with a nice diamond mounted in the center. For real Texas show, I guess. The rain had almost stopped and the clouds were parting, as I looked up the road, only to see the Red Sedan bearing down on us from the same direction it had just left.

With an undeveloped hand signal, both M#2 and myself cleared the fence and rolled through the mud to our now very familiar safe hiding place, as the mud-covered Red Sedan slid to a stop on the pavement right in front of the two big oak trees in what could be called, "The Killing Field."

The blonde opened her door and started immediately looking down at the ground, or, should I say, mud, for something she must have lost in the ordeal she had just suffered through. It appeared she was frantic and stepped off the highway right into a deep pool of blood stained water, with no regard for the fact that she was one shoe short. She made a small, quick circle toward the dumpster, as she sloshed through the mud, but turned away suddenly and continued to search the area right next to where the car was parked.

She was not holding the revolver any more. Since I didn't remember her retrieving it from the trunk of the car before she left, I did believe it could be what she was looking for.

The once good looking blonde, still with her ragged, drained appearance and no doubt in a pissed off mood, had reverted to just plain cussing old Ted for causing her this awkward time in her life, let alone the fact that she shot him three times just for his effort.

She stopped dead in her tracks. She must have stepped in the muddy shoe print of M#2. A look of disbelief coupled with deep concern crossed her still bleeding face as she adjusted to the real side of life, that those are not her footprints in the mud. If not, then whose footprints were they and where was the invader that had now interfered into this very personal side of her private life. She headed for the car and through the open door, retrieving the revolver that I thought was lost in the mud.

Looking right out in the pasture toward the brush where I was hiding, she yelled out, "Who are you, you SOB. Show yourself or I'll come out there and find you."

M#2 whispered in my ear, "Don't move a hair on your head. I'm sure as hell not ready to die here in what you call West Texas at the hands of a fired-up Blonde Bitch."

She fired into the wind and rain one wild shot high above the brush where I was lying and continued to cuss the unknown, the mud, and this, no doubt, much needed West Texas rainstorm and, also, I'm sure, the late Ted

Long for leaving her here with this predicament. She turned again toward the mud tire tracks and continued to look in and around this area for several more minutes, for what I don't know. I did know she was desperate to locate something she must have lost during her struggle with the death of the man now buried in the county dumpster just behind her.

She stopped again and turned toward where she fired the wild shot and screamed out as she did before, "Who are you? What do you want with me?" Then she quickly turned toward the car, got in and started the engine. She looked again over the pasture fence and right where I was lying and called out in a voice of panic, "I'll kill you, you SOB, if I ever find out who you are."

M#2 quietly remarked, "I believe she means it."

The car headed due east toward the Junction and turned left on the muddy road toward Spring Creek.

I continued to lay there for sometime, waiting to see if the Dove Creek Black Widow would come back for just one more look to see if she could find her lost belongings, whatever they might be, and also to see if she could get a shot at the mystery person who, without an invitation, had entered her private circle on this what must have been the worst day of her life.

To The Victor Belong The Spoils

After I don't know how long, I decided to investigate the crime scene again and to see if I could learn more about the late departed Ted Long. It appeared to me that someone, somewhere was going to miss Mr. Long, come sundown or come Monday when he didn't show up for work or whatever. At this very time, there were only three of us who knew where Mr. Ted Long was and where he was going, come "trash day" here in Irion County, Texas.

I climbed over the fence and started for the dumpster to finish the strip-andsearch program underway, when we were interrupted by the reappearance of the shooter. M#2 already had the wallet and class ring and now produced a silver identification bracelet from the left wrist of the corpse that bore the inscription, "To Ted, with all my love, Samantha." So just maybe, the ex-sweetheart was Samantha somebody from somewhere around here.

M#2 said, "Captain, she was driving a late model two-door Oldsmobile 98 hardtop and, as you know, it is red all over, inside and out. The license plate number was FWT 958 and I do believe that's just down the road where we met Tommy in that town you call Angelo. So if you think you need to meet her, I bet she's not going to be too hard to find. Let's just real quick go looking for a beat up blonde with her clothes torn off and one eye swollen closed and a nice deep cut just above her left eye. If there is a Red Sedan parked nearby with a 38-caliber bullet hole in the roof, I bet you two bucks it's her. She's not going to heal up for a month or so. What do you suggest we do for a proper introduction?"

"That's enough cute remarks, M#2," I retorted. "Let's get the hell out of here and head for the house and go through this stuff and figure out just what we are going to do."

M#2 came right back, "We, hell. You are the Captain and you started this whole mess, once you walked away from here with Old Ted's personal things in your pocket. You stopped being a witness to a shooting and now have become a person of importance. I think it's called harboring the enemy, that is, if you go without reporting this cold-blooded murder to the locals within the next ten minutes."

I started to move away from the dumpster and looked down to see just how deep the mud was when I noticed something sort of shiny on the left side of one of my combat boots' large, noticeable footprints. I reached down and picked at the spot where the shiny object first appeared and to my great surprise, I came up holding a diamond necklace. Not just any old diamond necklace, but one mounted in a gold frame, looped into a gold chain that had been broken at the catch.

M#2 said, "Do you think the Black Widow came back here to get her shoe, or could it have been this stack of diamonds?"

WHAT TO DO NEXT

When we got back to the ranch house, that is, me and the tacky Marine second person that always seems to interfere with good judgment, I noticed the rain had at last stopped. Now that I had some clear thinking time, I needed to make a few decisions as to what to do.

Do I want to play some sort of part in these lovers' quarrel, or should we say, murder, or should I just get in my truck and head over to El Dorado and have a talk with the sheriff?

M#2 spoke right up with another most profound statement. "Are you nuts or have you just gone plain stupid. This murder you saw is now over an hour old and you let the Blonde Bitch get away even after she shot at you, and now you are sitting in your kitchen two miles from the killing field and just starting to go through the dead man's personal items you willfully stole from his person right out of his funeral box. Captain, I believe this West Texas sun is starting to get to you. So, say we do decide to play along, what's in it for us? We have plenty of money and lots of ranch work to do and for damn sure sex is out of the question after the last affair Sweet Thing just finished off on. Just one more thing, what the hell are you going to do with that diamond?"

Ted's wallet revealed that he was in the oil business in some form or fashion, because he had several credit cards with memberships in petroleum clubs and oil and gas related businesses in several West Texas cities. His identification also indicated he was 37 years old. No record of him ever being in the armed services. The most important find was a wallet size picture of a classy looking blonde lady who had signed the back of the picture as, "I love you, Samantha."

M#2 spoke up, "Sure looks like the Dove Creek Black Widow to me; you know, the one who drives a Red Sedan."

I guess I was into my second rum and coke before I realized the sun was going down and it looked like I was committed to finding out more about Samantha Morgan and the death of the late Ted Long.

I thought back over this day's events and did my best to try to understand why I had become so interested in wanting to get involved in what appeared to be a lovers' quarrel, that had ended in murder or whatever we need to call it. I thought it was the intrigue and the mystery of this type of action that caused me to want to know more about the woman who drove off in the Red Sedan with murder on her breath.

No One Came To The Funeral

Trash pickup day was Monday, so Ted had another 24 hours to go unnoticed before he was to be deposited in the landfill just south of the city limits of El Dorado. I thought I would just drive over to the landfill on Monday and check out just what area the dumps were now taking place in. At least I'd know just what part of the landfill Ted would be located in; that is, if I ever needed to let someone know where Mr. Ted Long of Abilene, Texas, had gone. Things went off smooth on Monday and, sure enough, they took ole Ted over to the Irion County Landfill.

I kind of kept my eye on the Junction, as best I could, and to the best of my knowledge, Samantha didn't show up during my surveillance of the area. I felt like she came back several times, not looking for Ted, or her right shoe, but just maybe she was looking for a great diamond necklace.

Cooling Off Period

For the next two or three weeks I just worked on the many projects that the Dove Creek Ranch was demanding. Foremost was the completion of the house project so that some sort of normal cowboy life could take place without having to do so much in this primitive state of living. We needed furniture, a new refrigerator and stove and, for damn sure, some sheets and towels and just whatever else is needed so as to start to live like a real ranch owner, rather than a wetback.

It was Tuesday, about the last week in September and I was headed to Angelo for ranch supplies. M#2 had remained rather quiet since the burial of Ted Long, and more so, since the disappearance of the Red Sedan. Therefore, I felt like today I was sure going get a lot done. The first place I stopped was The Angelo Furniture Mart out on Beauregard, just as you come into town from the west.

As I entered the building, I noticed three rather good looking young women clustered around a large flat table, all looking at some sort of drawing. I didn't know what it was, but it sure did have their undivided attention.

The first one to look up was a very attractive dark complexioned gal with dark eyes and an arrangement of some of the most beautiful black hair streaming over her very trim shoulder and a most attractive body. Right out of the box came a very pleasant accented, "Can I help you? I'm Lucinda Morales."

I quickly stepped forward and shook her very small, dainty hand and before I could control my actions, I introduced myself as Captain Ron Heard of the USMC. I quickly tried to cover over that uncontrolled statement with "Or I'm just plain Ron Heard of the Dove Creek Ranch, and I'm here to buy a house full of furniture."

Lucinda lit up like a roman candle and so did the other two who up to this point had never even given me a look-see.

M2# climbed out of his shell and got right in my ear and said "Captain, the little blonde one is none other than The Dove Creek Black Widow. Note the remains of a scar over her left eye and can't you tell her face and left cheek are still somewhat blue and swollen?" He went on and on with, "Look, she has on two shoes, and I wonder if her breast is still sore. She's not carrying a 38 revolver and for sure no diamond necklace around that thin trim neck that should have a hangman's noose firmly attached just above her Adam's Apple. What are we going to do?"

"Nothing, get out of here and leave this be," I said.

The second young lady with red hair and lots to go with it, reached out her hand and introduced herself as Cherry

Longwell and right behind her, Samantha Morgan reached out for my hand and cheerfully said, "Hi, I'm Samantha Morgan. Did I hear you say you are a rancher and want a house full of furniture?"

"Yes, Ma'am, you did, and I think this sweet little Lucinda can handle all my needs."

After a little more conversation about the ranch and what it was called and that it was located halfway between Spring Creek and El Dorado and that I had only been there several months, Lucinda stepped in and suggested we go look at furniture. And so we did.

M#2 again started ragging me about, "She's just standing there flat-footed watching us. I can almost hear her brain telling her; Have I ever met him? If so, where and why do I feel his presence so powerfully over me?"

After about an hour with the lovely Lucinda, I had picked out a rather plain but ranch style bedroom suite and a few tables and lamps.

On the spur of the moment, I decided to ask Lucinda to come out to the ranch tomorrow when the crew delivered the furniture and go room to room with me and help decide just what else I needed.

As we went back to the office area where we started, I counted out two thousand dollars and laid it down on the table right in front of Cherry and Samantha and said, "This will be a down payment on what I now have and what else I need to get after tomorrow when you come to the ranch. I'll stand good for that also.

I then peeled off another $100.00 and asked Lucinda to get us and the delivery crew some great eats for lunch tomorrow, because I didn't have a refrigerator, but I would by this time tomorrow.

Needless to say, all three of the charming looking, fresh young women were a little starry eyed at my humble presence. For damn sure, Samantha looked me over from head to toe trying her best to place me, as if where she might have met me.

As I left The Angelo Furniture Mart through the front door, I looked back to see all three beauties getting ready to explode outright about just who the hell is this Captain Heard and is he married and did you notice at times he seems to be talking to himself.

Cherry said, "If I were him and owned a ranch and had all that money. I'd talk to myself, too."

THE PLOT STARTS HERE

The furniture crew and Miss Lucinda showed up at the Dove Creek Ranch the next day at around 10 a.m. and within an hour the bedroom furniture was unloaded and assembled in what I now call "The Captain's Room."

It was almost noon, so Lucinda took her basket of goodies and a bottle of red wine out to the back patio and the four of us sat on the wall of a planter box and ate lunch, cowboy style. The two boys finished up and told Lucinda they were headed back to Angelo and asked if she could make it on her own, since she had driven out alone in her little Ford Mustang.

After the boys left, Lucinda and I just stayed out in the patio for a spell and kind of introduced ourselves to each other. Lucinda told me about her being raised in far West Texas out around Van Horn, where her family owned and operated a dry goods store, and that she had spent the better part of her life working around dry goods and furniture.

She had gotten a scholarship for tennis to Angelo State College in 1968, but she majored in criminal science and law enforcement classes like that and had been out of college for the last year.

She went on to say she had met Samantha Morgan and Cherry Longwell about six months ago. Through this friendship, she learned that Samantha, who was several years older, had been married and divorced from a well-to-do oil man. With the large settlement money, she and Cherry had then formed a partnership and started The Angelo Furniture Mart.

It was interesting for me to know a little more about Samantha and that she had already been married and divorced.

M#2 jumped in, "Big deal, that doesn't tell us a damn thing about her and the late Ted Long."

We toured the rest of the house and Lucinda took notes on just what else the place needed to make it into a full-blown ranch house. I told her to pick out what I needed and that I would stop by the Furniture Mart on my next trip to Angelo and decide on what she had picked out. I gave her $500.00 more and asked her to get me enough sheets and towels and stuff like that.

By this time, it was almost 3 o'clock and I suggested she better get started back to Angelo. For a minute I got the feeling she just wasn't ready to go, but as she was walking out the door, she turned around and quickly kissed me on the cheek and said what a great day she had, could we do it again sometime; after all, it's my turn to tell her about who I am and where I came from.

M#2 said, "Hell yes, how about tomorrow and you bring your swimming suit or come without it and we will all go for a swim in the big cement tank that is just out back of the house."

I agreed, "Sure, let's do it again someday soon and I'll drive you around the ranch so you can see just how we West Texas cowboys handle ourselves."

THE PLOT THICKENS

Each day here at the Dove Creek Ranch began with my trying my best to decide just what I needed to do to make this great dream work. If I did come up with a good program, just how in the hell was I going to get it started.

I needed to start thinking about buying some cows, or sheep, or both, if I was going to be a rancher.

I started spending more time in El Dorado so that I could get to know the ranchers who lived in and around these parts. I figured this would help me learn more about what kind of livestock worked best around Dove Creek Ranch.

There is an old Sinclair Service Station just as you come into town from the south that is owned by Hot Shot Williams and his little brother, Charlie. This seemed to be the hangout for all us ranchers and it soon became obvious that Hot Shot could get you almost anything you needed wholesale, even if you soon found out you didn't need it that bad.

This Saturday, being October the 9th, soon proved to be one of those days where maybe you should have stayed home and minded your own business. Hot Shot, Charlie, and some of the locals, ranchers and some town folks, were out back of the station examining a trailer pulled by a pickup with what first appeared to be a junked car or, you might say, a wrecked car that Charlie had bought at a car auction in Ft. Worth, thinking it would be a great deal and, no doubt, a bargain.

Charlie fancied himself as a trader and whenever he could make a buck, he was always ready, but not always capable of coming up with the cash that he needed to finish out on his newest venture. Seems he bought the wrecked Red Oldsmobile Sedan for around $3,500.00 through an insurance agency at the auction and he and his car repair friend from Odessa, being just 125 miles east of here, were going to put the car back together and then sell it for upwards to $16,000.00.

However, after his friend got through with the repair estimates and the money was needed up front to get started, Charlie's big deal went south, due to a lack of available capital and, of course, Hot Shot wanted his share of the money already spent back in his pocket.

Just as I was starting to focus on the wrecked Red Sedan that was parked right in front of me, M#2 again got right up in my ear and said, "Captain, are you asleep at the wheel or can't you see that there wrecked Red Sedan once belonged to the Dove Creek Black Widow? I bet you $100.00 there is a bullet hole just off a little from the center in the roof of that vehicle."

Just about that time Charlie said, "Ron, you sure would look good in this fancy car, once it's fixed up. You might even find yourself a fresh, young wife, if you drove slow enough through Angelo."

Before I could get a good grip on myself, I said, "How much was the bid to complete the restoration and, Charlie, just what do you want to make you happy and to get out from under this deal?"

Before Charlie could respond to my question, big brother Hot Shot motioned to Charlie to come over his way for a family conference. Hot Shot stepped up and with his trading shoes on and his sharpened pencil over his ear, he said without hesitation, "Charlie will take $4,500.00 cash to get out and you will need to make your own deal with

Fred Strickland's Body Shop over to Odessa. Here is his phone number."

By this time everyone was looking at me as if I was insane and, no wonder, why would a fellow who just paid almost $1,500,000.00 cash for the Old Tom Tyler Ranch buy a wrecked car? I told Charlie and Hot Shot that I'd have to give it some thought and just maybe I could use a nice looking Red Sedan and that I'd get back to them in a day or two.

As I was getting ready to drive off, Hot Shot came out to the pickup and said, "Charlie will deliver the car over to Odessa as part of the $4,500.00 and I think Fred said he would fix it like new for around $6,500.00."

Without thinking, I said, "Ok, Hot Shot, just bring the car out to the ranch and when I get some time, Charlie and I can run it over to Odessa or wherever I can get it repaired for the best buck."

Hot Shot turned to Charlie and said, "Take the car out to Ron's ranch and leave it till he's ready to have it repaired. And don't charge him for the use of the trailer and be sure to get your money."

On the way back to the ranch, M#2 kept saying, "Captain, just what do you have in mind about that Red Sedan and Ms. Samantha Morgan?"

Looks Like Winter's Coming

It had been almost three weeks since I had last stopped off at The Angelo Furniture Mart and met the sweet, little Lucinda Morales. I was overdue for this appointment and the approval of her choices for the rest of the ranch house furniture that I had asked her to start working on.

As I walked into the big front room of the Furniture Mart, all three ladies in waiting greeted me in a very warm and, I must say, enjoyable appearance, this being my second introduction to their store. Lucinda was first in line and I got a sweet kiss on the cheek and a slight hug. I'm sure this was done to warn off the other two sweet things that were as surprised as I was to this grandstand reception from Lucinda.

We all exchanged greetings and right out of the hat, Samantha started to talk about the ranch as if she had been there with Lucinda and she more or less seemed to invite herself out to the ranch to inspect the choice and placement of furniture.

I didn't respond to her intentions, so I turned to Lucinda and said, "Well, good looking, what have you in store for me today?"

After about an hour of going from exhibition rooms to picture galleries, it seemed I had seen or heard enough about furniture to fill several ranch houses. We settled up on the living room and all the kitchen requirements and then Lucinda promised by the next week she would have all the furniture inhouse and ready to be delivered to the ranch and then we could decide on what to do about the other two bedrooms and whatever odds and ends I still might need.

This sounded perfect and was sure to fit in with the plan I had now come up with so as to introduce the Red Sedan back into the world of Samantha Morgan.

Just like the last time, we ended back in the main room and Lucinda started immediately to figure the furniture bill to date. It came to $5,285.00 including the $2,000.00 I had left the time before as a deposit. I again counted out $3,285.00 in cash while all three ladies watched again in awe, no doubt wondering where in the hell did this guy with all the cash come from.

I told Lucinda I had applied for phone service and the hook-up was to be ready in a day or so and informed her what the number would be. Now she could call before she and the crew came with the second load of furniture.

I then turned to Cherry and Samantha and said, "If you ladies need me for anything, please just give me a call at the ranch. It will be easier to reach me in the evenings."

Both of these beauties seemed surprised at my statement and I'm sure both wondered just what in the hell that comment was all about. They weren't by themselves. I was also a little confused at my own actions.

M#2 chimed in, just as I was leaving the Mart, and asked me just what I had in mind trying to involve these three good looking women in our lives at a time when we could be headed for real trouble.

Lucinda came out to the pickup and asked if she could come out to the ranch sometime on her own and get that tour I had promised her just before she left for Angelo the last time she was there.

I said, "Sure, you're welcome anytime. Fact is, I've missed seeing you and this will give us time to get to know each other a little better." This was all she needed to hear. She once again reached over and gave me kiss on the cheek and said, "I missed seeing you too."

Meanwhile, Back At The Ranch

I still had in mind to get some sort of livestock for the ranch before winter set in. That very day when I was up to the mail boxes on County Road CC-26, I had a chance to visit with my neighbor, Jack Fields of the Circle 6 Ranch. Jack and his family owned and operated one of the biggest cow/calf ranches in the county. I went over my needs with Jack, thinking his information would be about the best ranching and cattle grazing data I could get.

Right up front, Jack suggested that I lease out my pasture land to an outside rancher who would put a certain amount of cattle on The Dove Creek Ranch for grazing at $4.00 a head per month for the next six months, or until next spring. The owner of the cattle would look after the herd and all Dove Creek would need to do would be to keep up the waterings and fences. Jack went on to say that this would give me time to get myself realigned back into the cattle business.

Before I headed back to the ranch, I had made a deal with the Circle 6 Ranch to graze 150 head of open heifers through the winter and up into the spring of 1976. As it turned out, Jack's two boys would be looking to the heifers and they would want to keep a few horses at my headquarters, so as to saddle up a couple times a week and check their cattle. They would bring an extra horse and tack for me, so I could go with them, when I took the notion.

The cattle arrived three days later and Bob and John Fields came with the cattle and we all sat down and mapped out the pastures that the heifers would start grazing in. It took another two days to get the heifers settled down and, for sure, I did enjoy getting to ride out with the two Field boys, as we went from pasture to pasture with just so many head.

M#2 was doing a lot of complaining about this new type of work I was enjoying, where you spend most of the day riding horseback and no time at all trying to figure out the answers to some of the questions that needed to be dealt with, such as, what to do with sweet Lucinda and the wrecked Red Sedan. You know, the one with the bullet hole in the roof that I now had parked at the ranch. And let's not forget Samantha Morgan and her once departed lover, Mr. Ted Long, and for damn sure, her beautiful diamond necklace.

About the end of the month, Lucinda called and said she had the next day off, which was Friday, and could she come for a visit to The Dove Creek Ranch. My answer was, "Sure thing. Why not come on out and spend the weekend and we can tour the ranch and check the cattle."

A Pretty Gal And A Lonesome Cowboy

Lucinda showed up, as planned, on Friday and brought along some sandwiches and a six-pack of Lone Star Beer. It was just my kind, cold and long-neck style.

M#2 asked me right up front, "Did she bring her swim suit or will we all have to go skinny dipping later on this afternoon?"

Once again we moved out back to the patio in the cool of the giant oak trees and started in on our picnic lunch. Right up front Lucinda asked me to tell her about myself and how I got this great ranch. She also wanted to know if I realized that sometimes I seemed to be talking to myself? Could this have been caused from being in the Vietnam War?

I went through a story I had been rehearsing for this event that I knew was going to happen, whenever Lucinda and I found ourselves alone. I went into a long and fearless story about my U.S. Marine Corps days and how I had been wounded just prior to my leaving Vietnam.

This seemed to get her attention and she continued to ask me questions about the war and just what role I had played during my full term in the Marines.

As to the ranch, I told her my father's sister, who lived Back East, had left me a sizeable amount of money that she had accumulated in the stock market over her lifespan of some 70 odd years. When I got back to the United States, I claimed the money, paid the tax and came back to West Texas looking for something to do with the rest of my life. As it happened, I showed up in Spring Creek the day of the auctioning off of the Tom Tyler Ranch and so I just bought it and here I am.

Lucinda backed off from asking me any more questions about who, what and why. However it seemed to me she left the conversation about the money open for future discussion.

We spent the entire afternoon driving around the ranch just looking at the many different places and sites that this 11,000-acre ranch had to offer. As we turned toward the house, we passed through pasture #2 and I pointed out the large dirt tank just down below the two great live oak trees that all the kids in this area seemed to think they could come and trespass through my property to go skinny dipping in, any time they wanted to.

For some reason she ask me to stop and take a look at the old swimming hole that seemed to be so popular with all the kids. So we did, but right off, I felt like she was not as interested in the old dirt tank as she was the two hundred yard trail back up the hill to the hole in the fence and, of course, the two dumpsters and the other two corresponding live oak trees on the other side of the fence.

M#2 jumped in and reminded me that we were now back in the Killing Field area with a complete stranger who seemed to want to, shall we say, "check the area out", and just for what reason?

I explained to Lucinda that this was an area known as The Junction and, according to the Sheriff over to El Dorado, teenagers had been coming over here for as long as he could remember. Perhaps as a teenager he himself used to come over this way at night to drink some beer and do a little spooning.

We came right up to the fence that I had climbed over several times during the final phase of the disappearance of The Late Ted Long. Lucinda's interest in this particular spot gave me some concern, but I thought I'd just play as casual as I could until I could learn just what her big interest was in wanting to know anything about The Junction area.

We went back to the pickup and turned toward the ranch house. I hoped that this might be the end of Lucinda Morales's interest in such an isolated place on a cattle ranch some 45 miles from her home base. We arrived back at the headquarters about 6:30 in the evening and I suggested we drive over to El Dorado to the Ranch House Cafe and partake of their Friday night special of fresh catfish and corn dogs.

After a great meal, we dropped in on the one-and-only nightspot in this whole county. That was a place called, "The Seldom Inn", which was a honky-tonk bar and dance floor and, for sure, a live three-piece western band.

Right off, several of the locals took notice of this beautiful, little Mexican gal I was sporting around and, in fact, some of my new-found friends came over to ask Lucinda if she would care to dance around the floor a few turns with them. The only way to stop this interference was to either dance with her myself or head on back to the ranch and see just what was to happen the rest of this rather pleasant day.

Reluctantly I said, "Let's head back to the ranch and see if some of those long neck beers are still cool enough to drink."

M#2 got right up in my ear and explained that we were for sure passing up a chance to have some real action with some of the local punks over just who this little Senorita belongs to. Had I completely forgot about all my Marine Training as to

Meanwhile, back at the ranch, yes, the beers were still cold, so we moved inside, because the mosquitoes were out in full force and because I had no furniture yet to sit on. We just moved into the Captain's Room and stretched out on the bed.

Needless to say, the rest of the night was outstanding. This beautiful little Mexican gal was hotter than a pistol and it wasn't long before I was plumb tuckered out and fell asleep with her right next to me with my arm around her.

The next morning it was raining. That kind of put a damper on this Saturday for any outdoors activity. About noon Lucinda packed up her things and said she might as well go on back to Angelo where she was sure there would be plenty for her to do.

I reluctantly let her have her way and we made plans to get together sometime soon in Angelo for a night on the town, where there was hopefully not going to be so much male interference.

She hoped the rest of the ordered furniture would be in this week, so she would be seeing me again right here at the headquarters house.

Just as she was leaving, she put her arms around me and said, "I still don't know very much about you and your Marine Corps days. Perhaps some day I'll let your finish your life story." She gave me a great big kiss on the lips and whispered, "You were great last night. Let's do it again when you aren't so sleepy!"

M#2 also whispered in my other ear, "Captain, what in the hell is going on with this chick and why does she need to know so much about us? Please explain to me just what her interest is in the Killing Field. For sure I thought we were through telling our life story yesterday at noon, or did you indicate there was something else you wanted to lie to her about?"

What's Going On?

Later that day after the rain had stopped and when I went up to the mail boxes, I quickly noticed that Lucinda's car tracks when leaving the ranch earlier this day had turned left toward The Junction on CC-26 rather than going right toward El Dorado, the better highway route to Angelo. I followed her muddy tracks two miles east right to the dumpsters below The Junction, where she stopped and got out of her car.

From here she tracked herself through the mud over to the dumpsters where the hole in the fence had once again been cut to allow trespassing onto my ranch, most likely to the dirt tank-swimming hole. It appears she just stopped, once she reached the fence, and then must have looked over the entire area from where her car was parked on the road.

M#2 said, "Just what in the hell is this sweet, little Latino girl doing up here at the Killing Field? Just what could she know about this area, unless girlfriend Samantha has sometime or another told her about this great spot over in Irion County known as 'Lovers' Hide Out'."

She then got back into her car and turned left at The Junction and went on into Spring Creek on CC-26.

M#2 jumped in again and said, "This babe has been out here before, how else would she have known about the back road to Spring Creek?"

I sat back in the pickup and tried to gather my thoughts around today's events and how Lucinda first acted when we drove up through pasture #2 and got what I thought was her first look at The Junction and the hole in my fence and, for sure, the two dumpsters that had been the disposal site for the late Mr. Ted Long.

I decided from this point on to watch myself a little closer when I had any dealings with Lucinda Morales. She now seemed to be someone other than the sweet, little Mexican girl from Van Horn, Texas, but for the life of me, I just couldn't put anything together at this time.

At about that time, I remembered the Red Sedan parked out back behind the ranch house and just what would have been her reaction to the Dove Creek Ranch's having that particular car sitting right there in plain view. I now needed to set up a happening on her next trip to the ranch, where she would have a chance at a good look at The Black Widow's get-away vehicle. I was already programmed to see just how she was going to react to Samantha's wrecked Red Sedan.

The rest of the week went by rather fast, since I was spending as much time as I could with the two Field boys checking their cattle. Then as we were unsaddling our horses on Friday, Bob Field said in sort of a joking manner, "I hear over to Hot Shot's place that you sure had you a good looker over to the Seldom Inn last Friday night and that most of the boys sure wanted to share her with you. Bill Reynolds who used to work for The Texas Department of Public Safety in the Car Theft Division mentioned he thought he knew the little Mexican gal you were with, because she sure favors one of the gals who used to work in the Narcotics Division of the Texas Rangers."

M#2 almost threw a shoe before he could get right up front in my face and tell me, "Now look what you gone and done. We now have the Texas Rangers looking at us, and haven't I heard they always get their man, or is that the Canadian Mounties?"

CAREFUL, AS SHE GOES

With all the new developments taking precedence over my wanting to be just a plain West Texas Cowboy, I had little time to finish up on some of the projects I had started last summer. It was now November 2, 1975, and tomorrow Lucinda Morales would be due at the ranch with some more of the ranch house furniture and, for sure, I was going to give her a chance to discover the Red Sedan.

I would need to pay very close attention to her reaction, because it now appeared that she could be someone other than a Furniture Mart Sales Lady and just who or what is she turned on to? I felt sure it had to have something to do with Samantha and some of her travels along these West Texas Highways. Could she or the late Ted Long have been running dope from Mexico into West Texas? After all, Del Rio, Texas, and the Mexican border were only about 125 miles south of Angelo.

Lucinda and the furniture express showed up at the ranch on Wednesday about noon. We had our lunch out back and as soon as we finished, the crew unloaded and assembled all the new furniture. Boy, this old ranch house was starting to sure enough look like a first class ranch house. The crew packed up and headed for Angelo, leaving Lucinda to drive back to town whenever she was ready.

I sat down in the front room to sort of get used to all the new things, while Lucinda washed up the few things we used during the lunch break. It was so nice and cool and pleasant in the big living room that I must have dozed off. I must have needed this little nap, because I hadn't been asleep for long when I heard Lucinda calling my name in a rather forceful manner.

I jumped up and headed for the kitchen only to see Lucinda out back standing right in front of the wrecked Red Sedan. She looked like she had seen a ghost and was still calling for me when I got to her side. Right off she said, "Where did you get Samantha's car and why did you wreck it?"

Without showing too much concern, I said, 'Samantha who? This car now belongs to me. I just got through paying Charlie Williams $4,500.00 cash and he pulled the car over to the ranch and left it right here about two weeks ago."

The next statement was, "Yes, this very vehicle was right here last week when you came to spend the weekend with me and for some reason you must have missed seeing it at that time."

By this time Lucinda was trying to open the driver's side door and was climbing up on the trailer to get into the car. I grabbed her arm and pulled her gently back down to ground level so I could look her right in the face and then ask her, "Just what in the hell is your interest in this old wrecked car?"

Lucinda was almost crying when she blurted out that several months ago for some reason Samantha hadn't shown up for work on a Monday and had decided to take off the next work week. She had ended up in Austin where she had traded in the Red Sedan for a brand new black BMW sports model, the one she was driving now.

Seems that Samantha had promised Lucinda that if she ever traded or wanted to sell the Red Sedan that Lucinda was to have first option to buy the car. That just didn't happen and there never was another word said about her spur of the moment trading off of her Red Sedan. Lucinda then calmed down and hinted she couldn't wait until she could get back to the store and be the first to inform Samantha Morgan that her once treasured little Red Sedan was now back in the area, wrecked, soon to be repaired, and now belonged to none other than Captain Ron Heard of the Dove Creek Ranch.

The rest of the afternoon Lucinda seemed to be preoccupied with her thoughts, no doubt the Dove Creek Ranch in general, and all that had confronted her at this location in the last two months since we first met.

Without another word, she jumped up and said, "I better be getting on back to Angelo and tend to some of the work that's been piling up on my desk so Samantha won't have cause to concern herself with the extra time I have been spending out here at the ranch with you." At that, out the front door she went without even a goodbye kiss or "I'll be seeing you again real soon."

M#2 calmly watched her drive off in her little mustang and then commented, "That ain't the last time we're going to see that little dark eyed secret agent."

As I expected, two days later I had a call from none other than Samantha Morgan, demanding to know where and how I had come up with her Red Sedan.

First off, just to let her know whose show this was going to be, I said, "Hold on, Samantha, it's not your car and I don't have to discuss anything about my having this Red Sedan out here on my ranch with you or anyone else who seems to have a past or present interest in this junked 98 Oldsmobile."

This didn't seem to phase her one bit, for she just kept on ragging me about the fact that I hadn't told her at our last meeting that I now owned her old car.

I decided to move the conversation into another level so I just casually said, "Were you hurt very badly when you wrecked the car? I don't see how you kept from cutting your head off from the way the right window shield is caved in. After looking over the car I think for sure someone sustained some very bad cuts because the smell on the inside of the car when it has been shut up and has not been open to fresh air ventilation gives off a dead-like smell, much like old dried blood. I know this smell from having been around a lot of wounded Marines over in Vietnam."

There was nothing but silence on her end of the phone. I had to say, "Are you still there, Samantha?" At last a greatly subdued voice came back over the phone and said, "Yes, Ron. I was hurt in the accident and that's the very reason I traded the car in. I now realize that decision was wrong and selfish of me not to discuss this action with Lucinda, but I guess I was under so much pain and stress that I just wasn't thinking properly. Please forgive me for bringing up this car matter to you, a good friend, in such a crude manner.

She said, "You are going to have the car repaired and perhaps sell it to the highest bidder; is that so?"

M#2 stood flatfooted right in front of me and said, "Captain, that Black Widow and her lying story about her wrecking her car is all bullshit and you for one better realize she is capable of biting her death wish again and I do believe its going to be our turn."

I now responded, "Samantha, thanks for the call. I hope this car issue is closed for good. After I get it fixed, I might just drive it out to California and give it to a beautiful red headed nurse that took extra good care of me while I was in the Navy Hospital recovering from some wounds I received while serving with the Marines in Vietnam. But whatever, it's no concern of yours or Lucinda's."

WHERE TO GO FROM HERE

Once again I was left alone with my contentment, and certainly my thoughts, as to just what was next on the agenda: what to do with or about Lucinda, due to the fact that I now believed, after talking to Bill Reynolds about his having known Lucinda when she worked for the Narcotics Division of the State of Texas, that she no doubt was an undercover agent and was tracking someone in this area of West Texas. For what, I just hadn't figured out yet.

Let's not forget about Samantha Morgan, the lying little cute blonde who I saw kill her lover in cold blood and now she had wormed her way into my side of the action by stating she wrecked her Red Sedan and then traded it off for another car.

That we know is a big fat lie, because Charlie Williams talked with the insurance man when he bought the car at the auction and found out the car belonged to and was wrecked by a teenager from Austin who came from a very uptown and rich Austin family. To top this fact off as true, his name, being Wayne Hobbs, was on the title that was issued by Austin BMW Sports Cars.

It must have been a new title because Samantha Morgan's name was not anywhere on the Chain of Title. She got that done, for sure, when she traded it in and they must have detailed it out, but just didn't get all the smells out.

Let's not forget Mr. Ted Long, who, as far as I knew, was still resting in peace at the Irion County Landfill. M#2, once again, had a few leftout facts to register with me and started with our still having all the personal items of the late Mr. Ted Long over at the ranch house and that we should get rid of them, in case someone like Lucinda were to find them. And of course there was the beautiful diamond necklace, still draped on the faucet handle in the bathroom shower, for whatever reason I hadn't figured out.

The next time I was in Angelo, I stopped at The Furniture Mart and inquired about Lucinda, who I hadn't heard from in over three weeks. Much to my surprise and disappointment, Cherry Longwell informed me that Lucinda did not work there anymore. "I heard just yesterday that she had moved all her things out of her apartment and was headed back to Austin, where I believe she had come from."

M#2 spoke up and informed me that Lucinda's sudden dismissal was sure fast and furious and for sure she hadn't given us a going away notice. "So what's going on, Captain? I hope we won't wake up some morning and Miss Lucinda and a line of Texas Narcotics Vehicles are coming through our gate for an unannounced visit."

Cherry went on to inform me that she would be happy to take over Lucinda's account with Dove Creek Ranch and for sure finish up on getting the ranch house furnished before cold weather set in. I looked Cherry over and, without even a stutter, I said, "Sure, why not? I suggest you come out to the ranch and go over what's been done so far and let's get this deal over with."

About that same time, Samantha came into the big room from the back and was surprised to see me standing there, talking to Cherry. Before I could greet her, she jumped right into the middle of my conversation with Cherry and offered to help me finish up getting my ranch house completely furnished.

Cherry said, "That's already taken care of, Samantha, but why don't you come along with me one day this week and we will both go out to the Dove Creek Ranch and see what was so fascinating to Lucinda, other than ranch furniture."

M#2 said, "Here it comes. Trouble in twos and I know you can't handle both of these darlings, so I'll take the Red Head and you hook up with the Dove Creek Black Widow."

It's Getting Closer To The Time

Cherry and Samantha arrived at the ranch on Friday just before lunch and, to my surprise, brought a lunch basket and some cold beer. I suggested we just sit in the dining room, because I still didn't have any patio furniture and it for sure wasn't too comfortable sitting on the rock wall at high noon in the full sunlight.

Right off, Samantha asked if I still had the Red Sedan and could she have a quick look at it before she left. I responded, "Sure. Let's all eat this great lunch and then we can go out back and look at the car." I added, "Not much to see, but what the hell, let's give it a once over just for old time's sake."

The lunch meal was nice and pleasant, but I couldn't stop wondering just what had happened to Lucinda and why she hadn't bothered to even give me a call. For some reason I thought we had a little something nice going on between us, but I guess that was my shortcoming, because it appeared she was more interested in checking out this area, and not me.

The lunch meal being over, we all headed out back to view the mysterious Red Sedan, as it still stood firmly tied down on Hot Shot's trailer. I noticed right off Samantha's attitude changed, once she got to the car, and I do believe she was ready to cry when Cherry said, "For God's sake, Samantha, how did you keep from getting killed in the wreck?"

Before Samantha could answer and to keep her story more or less to her making, I quickly said, "Looks like this car has been wrecked twice and repaired only once, according to what looks like new paint and repair work on the driver's side."

Samantha was quick to reply to Cherry that when she hit the lamppost, the damage was on the driver's side and not on the passenger side, where all the damage was now located.

After some more general discussion about her mishap with the lamppost in Austin, Samantha asked if she could get inside the car and look for a necklace she might have lost at the time of the accident. I again went through the same drill that I had already repeated to Lucinda that the car being up on the trailer as it is now would be impossible to open either door, due to the lack of clearance between the door and the rail of the trailer. This statement was not good enough for Samantha, because she had already began to pull on the driver's side door with every intention of getting inside of her old car, but with no results, because she could not possibly squeeze herself through that small opening.

About that time we all got a whiff of the stale air that had been trapped inside the sun baked car for these last two weeks. There was no doubt that Samantha was more shocked than either Cherry or myself, due to the smell that must have brought back some powerful memories of that horrible Saturday morning when she and Mr. Ted Long had parted company under such painful terms.

Samantha was transfixed for a few minutes, but when she recovered, she turned to me and said, "Will you please, if at all possible, make an effort to look through the car and see if you might find this diamond necklace my ex-husband gave me on our second anniversary?" I responded in a very positive manner and said that not only would I look for it, but I would instruct the car repair people to pay close attention to the interior of the car, as they no doubt would have to rip out the floorboard carpet to replace it with new, due to whatever was causing that bad smell.

M#2 got right up in my face and said, "Just what do you have in mind? For sure you're not dumb enough to give that great necklace back to this arrogant blonde bitch, are you?" The rest of the day went rather fast and it was decided that Cherry would now add some patio furniture to the ever-growing list of items from The Furniture Mart.

The two girls both seemed ready to get back to Angelo, so we said our goodbyes and I saw them out to Samantha's new BMW Sports Car.

Cherry said, "I'll be coming out with the rest of the furniture when I can get it all assembled, and I would hope I could have that tour over the ranch that Lucinda often spoke of."

Nothing But The Facts

Four or five days later, I called up Fred Strickland's repair shop in Odessa and made arrangements to take the car in on Thursday, November the 7th. Charlie and I pulled the car over to Odessa and I made a cash deal with Fred to do all the repairs for just a little under $6,000.00.

I also told him that there were a few misplaced things, no doubt hiding somewhere in the interior of the car, and that I would pay a cash bonus to anyone who found anything like jewelry. Prior to taking the car over to Odessa, I had managed to work the class ring of Mr. Ted Long under the front seat on the driver's side. I felt sure they would find the ring and return it for the cash bonus, whereas, I knew for sure if I hid the diamond necklace and it was found, it would never be returned, regardless of the bonus.

Cherry called the ranch several days later and informed me that all of the items ordered were now in the warehouse and as soon as the crew could get everything assembled, she would give me another call and bring everything out at one time. This sounded o.k. to me and it would give me a little time to think about how I was going to place Miss Cherry Longwell, if at all, in the loop, so to speak, and just who was she, anyway?

Fred Strickland from Odessa called on Friday and reported his crew had found a gold class ring of some kind and just how much bonus was I going to pay to the lucky worker. I said, "I'll kick in $100.00 cash. How do you want to receive it?" Fred went on to say, "Just leave the money with Hot Shot and when I'm over there one day next week, I'll bring the ring and leave it with him." This arrangement suited me fine.

Now I must decide how to work the ring into Cherry's upcoming visit to the ranch.

It's Time To Draw The Loop In Closer

I got over to Hot Shot's on Wednesday, just as Fred himself arrived from Odessa. The exchange was made and everything looked like it was going to work out smooth, until Charlie demanded to know just what I wanted with the ring and just how much was he going to get out of this deal, since he was the one who was smart enough to buy the car in the first place.

I reminded Charlie that I had paid him $4,500.00 cash for his entire interest in the car over three weeks ago and that was all I felt like he was entitled to. He didn't like it, but Hot Shot stepped in and informed Charlie that he was no longer involved in the trade on the Red Sedan.

No one asked me anything about the ring or how I knew it might have been in the car and what did I want with it anyway?

Cherry showed up on Friday and it didn't take the crew long to arrange the rest of the furniture and that included some great patio furniture that sure did look good out back. The crew packed up and left almost as fast as they had arrived. Seems they had other deliveries over to El Dorado. Cherry and I sat out back in the patio and drank a cold beer and spent an hour or so just getting to know each other. I already felt like this might turn out to be even better than the one night stand with the now gone Lucinda.

Out of the clear blue, Cherry said, "Did the car repair people find Samantha's high dollar diamond necklace yet?"

"No, but they did find something else. Hold on just a minute and I'll go see if I can find where I put it."

M#2 started out by saying, "Just what the hell are you going to do with that dead guy's ring that has already cost us 100 bucks and may go on to cost us this here West Texas ranch that you seem to be so proud of?"

When I retrieved the ring from the bathroom, I carried it out to the patio in the little plastic bag Fred had put it in. So I just pitched it out on the table right in front of Cherry. She nonchalantly picked up the small bag and began to look at the ring. Curiosity got the best of her so she opened the bag and took out the ring that was still rather dirty and began to look ever so closely at the insignia and inscription inside the ring band. Without hesitation or concern she read out loud, "Ted Long. Class of 1967." Cherry Longwell froze and her features seemed to turn to stone as she repeated out loud once again, "Ted Long. Class of 1967."

My response to her fright was that of great concern and I blurted out, "Cherry, what's wrong? You look like you have seen a ghost."

She didn't talk for a few minutes and her eyes filled up with tears. Her words, now that she seemed ready to talk, were hard to come by. In fact she started shaking and crying at the same time. I jumped up and went around to her chair and put my arm around her and tried my best to console her, as she continued to shake and lose control of her words.

At last she seemed to settle down somewhat and with a very shaky hand, she reached out and picked up the ring and once again read out loud, "Ted Long. Class of 1967." Cherry then looked up at me and said, "My sister, Rachel, is married to Ted Long's brother, Bob Long. Ted has been missing for several months without any explanation or personal contact with any of his family. His ex-wife Mary and their two young children are heart broken that their father hasn't come home, since he left on a business trip to West Texas around the first of September. Just what the hell was this ring doing in Samantha Morgan's Red Sedan and what did she have to do with Ted Long?"

At that moment she stood up and headed for the door with the ring in her hand. I said, "Hold on there just a second. You seem a little stressed out to be driving back to Angelo by yourself. And besides I want the ring. If you or anyone wants or needs this ring, they can contact me and I'll be glad to give them the whole story from start to finish on how I came in contact with the ring in the first place."

She dropped the ring on the floor and without another word went right to her car and drove off without so much as a smile or goodbye.

M#2 without holding back said, "Do you have any idea just what you have done by exposing the ring to Cherry Longwell?" He went on, "I suggest you gather up the remainder of the personal effects of the late Ted Long and let's dig a very deep hole somewhere out on this West Texas Ranch of ours and bury these items before you are, maybe, tempted to show off your stupidity again by giving his gold Rolodex watch to Samantha as a keepsake."

I was now aware as to the no doubt repercussions this sudden appearance of the missing Ted Long's ring was going to cause and, for sure, the officials whoever they are, would want to hear my story about the car and go over the car from top to bottom. They won't find anything tangible, but they might find bloodstains and, if they can be traced, it's all going to point right back to the Dove Creek Black Widow. What we needed to do was just keep a very low profile with little or no talking about anything and we would just see how the cookie would crumble.

That night back at the ranch house, I began to wonder just what Cherry might do when she figures out that her partner and best friend must of had some relationship with Ted Long this past summer and, if so, where did she meet him and how did she and the Red Sedan figure into the whereabouts of Mr. Ted Long?

I went on to speculate that perhaps Lucinda might have been checking up on Samantha or Cherry for some other reason, even if it wasn't dope trafficking out of Mexico. So why not bring Lucinda back into the loop and help her out with a few planted ideas that might give her some real purpose in her finding out about the Black Widow and the whereabouts of the late Mr. Ted Long. After all, it would be only proper to have his family know just what caused his disappearance in the first place and at least bring him home for a proper funeral.

M#2 continued to question me about my motive in my more or less pointing a finger toward Samantha. I thought about my reasoning and finally had to admit that Samantha Morgan was guilty of cold blooded murder, even if the original rendezvous had started out on a much softer note with what must have been two lovers looking for some Saturday morning excitement.

I went on to explain to M#2, that even though I hadn't first reported the tragic event, it was still my duty to let some of the facts surface that just might not have been discovered. Besides, I now wanted to be free from this entire mess that was almost taking over my getting back into the ranching business.

A New Plan

I thought I would start with the two dumpsters and bring them into focus as to how they had played a part in this event. So on Tuesday, I drove over to the landfill and asked to visit with the disposal team that worked The Junction area over between El Dorado and The Dove Creek Ranch. The project foreman indicated there were only two truck details in full service at this landfill and E.R. Montoya and his partner were the team that worked all the area east and south of El Dorado clear to the County line.

The foreman pointed Mr. Montoya out to me and I ambled over to his truck, which he and his partner were servicing at the time. After a few "coma estas" and a handshake, I asked E.R. if in the past month or two they had noticed any dead deer or wild hogs killed around the two dumpsters over by Dove Creek Ranch.

I went on to say that for sometime now strange things had been happening right around this area where a hole in my pasture fence continued to be opened, no matter how many times I wired it closed. I told him I felt like someone might be killing deer or hogs down by the water tank and then dragging them up to the dumpster to dress out and that no doubt then some of the leftover parts could have been thrown in the dumpster after they claimed all the good cuts of meat they wanted.

I said in a very positive voice that I wasn't sure this was going on, but if E.R. and his partner had ever seen any bones or hide in the dumpster that this would confirm my suspicions and perhaps I could get the Sheriff or Game Warden to pay a little closer attention to this area. E.R. responded that he didn't think that they had ever picked up any kind of dead animal that might have been deposited in the dumpster.

Just as I started to leave, Charles Torrez, E.R.'s partner said, "Several months ago after we dumped the dumpster, it's required by State and County policy that the dumpsters have to be sanitized at least twice a month, and for sure one time one of those dumpsters could have been used to discard some kind of animal leftovers, because the inside of the dumpster was covered with dried blood and we like to have never got it clean enough to pass inspection."

He went on to say that he had seen my new sign that said, "No hunting or fishing beyond this fence. All violators will be prosecuted." He thought that might stop some of the trespassing across my pasture to the dirt tank.

The next thing I wanted to do was to somehow reacquaint myself with Lucinda. That would require going into Austin and somehow seeing if I could locate her present place of employment. Better than that, I would just call Information and see if there was a new phone number for Lucinda Morales. And sure enough, there was.

I had most everything caught up at the ranch, so I took a few days' vacation and headed for Austin just to see if I could make contact with my old girlfriend, Lucinda Morales.

I arrived in Austin on a Thursday afternoon and the first thing I did was call her new number as given to me by Information. I rang her home phone and soon an answering service came on and reported that the persons living at this number were not in, but to leave my number and they might return the call at a later time. I left my motel and room number on the answering service and settled down for what I hoped was not going to be too long of a wait before Lucinda made the return call.

After several hours of stupid TV westerns, I decided to go down to the bar and have a Rum and Coke and try to figure out what I should do next. I was just about halfway down on my first drink, when who should walk right through the sliding door of the bar but Lucinda Morales. She was better looking than I ever remembered.

Her greeting was sharp and to the point, "Ron, just what the hell are you doing here in Austin and how did you get my phone number?"

Before she could say, "What do you want with me," I quickly said, "Cherry said she thought you moved to Austin and since I had some business over this way, I hoped I could find you, so I called Information and, for sure, your number is listed as L. Morales. So I gave it a ring and now, here you are."

"O.K., so you found me. Just what do you want with me anyway?"

"Hell, Lucinda. How about some explanation about you just up and leaving me waiting for you at the ranch. I thought we had something going, besides your selling me furniture."

She calmed down somewhat and then with no reason whatsoever, she said, "That red headed bitch fired me when she thought I had been going through some of the company records that didn't pertain to me or my line of work."

I responded, "Well, were you?"

Her reply was, "Damn sure I was and for sure it is my line of work. I already know you found out who I am from that dumb bastard Reynolds from over to El Dorado."

It's Time To Make A New Start

I finally got Lucinda to sit down and have an Old Fashion, in hopes she would get around to asking me just what's been going on in my world. Damn if she didn't jump right back into the middle of the loop.

She took a big drink and seemed to relax somewhat and then she demanded to know, "What did you do with the damn Red Sedan you had at the ranch last time I was out your way?"

So I told her about Cherry and Samantha both coming out to the ranch on the pretext of wanting to finish up the furniture needs of The Dove Creek Ranch. "You know, Lucinda, the account I had been paying and waiting on for the last two months."

Her response to that off the wall dig was, "I watched how you looked at that red headed bitch every time you came into the store. I bet you hoped you could get her in your big cowboy bed; you know, the one you tried to christen me in but fell short because you needed sleep."

After we got through cutting each other up in little pieces, I gave her the full story on Samantha and her reaction to seeing the car again. Then with a contrived concern in my voice, I went into great detail about not finding her high dollar necklace at the repair shop, but they did find a Texas A & M Class of 1967 ring under the front seat of the car during the repair job by Fred Strickland of Odessa. As it turned out later, the ring belongs to a Mr. Ted Long, whoever he is, and just wherever he has run off to, because he ain't been home to Abilene in over two months.

I could see she was showing great interest in this event, especially since it concerned Samantha Morgan and the now more than famous Red Sedan. Just as her detective brain started to kick in with a mouth full of questions, I told her about how her dear friend Cherry had showed up at the ranch by herself to deliver the last load of furniture.

When confronted with the ring that had been given to me by Mr. Strickland, she positively identified the ring as belonging to her sister's husband's brother and how she had gone into such a crying fit over just why in the hell was her partner of some four years hanging out with a man from Abilene, who had gone missing and what did she know about his disappearance.

It seemed no one had seen or heard from him in over two months or so and his ex-wife and two children were very disturbed over the sudden disappearance of Mr. Ted Long.

At this point in the discovery process being provided for Detective Lucinda Morales, M#2 whispered in my ear, "Big Boy, you have given this little Senorita enough facts and implications to choke a fat hog to death. Do you think she can handle this big of bite all at once? One more thing, Captain, The loop you want to get Lucinda back into may be the same loop Detective Morales puts around your neck."

My response was, "Damn right, she took the bait. Just look at those dark eyes searching me over to see if there is some way or reason I might be involved in this now great mystery that is somehow going to work its way through the Red Sedan, back to The Junction and the two dumpsters; you know, the same place Lucinda showed so much interest in."

The rest of the evening turned out to be a dud, especially after Lucinda began to talk about all the action that had surfaced around the ranch since she moved back to Austin. I felt like she was more than ready to get her police team more familiar with the Red Sedan and just who Mr.

Ted Long was and how did her old employer, Samantha Morgan, fit into whatever was going on around Dove Creek, and a few other questions she needed answers to.

M#2 jumped right back in my face and said, "Big deal, Marine. You seemed to have covered most of the bases with Lucinda, but for sure you missed the most important clue for her to discover and that is the blood the trash men had such a hard time cleaning out of the dumpster."

I responded, "No need to give her all the facts. She might figure she is being set up. I feel sure she will get around to the dumpsters once again and to the fact they do play a big part in whatever she was after in the first place and maybe she will tie the disappearance of that Texas Aggie into the whole package."

I left Austin the next day knowing full well that Detective Lucinda Morales would be calling on the Dove Creek Ranch in the near future.

On the way back to my ranch, M#2 reminded me, "We had never taken the ring in to Samantha's place of work and presented it to her as found in her once owned Red Sedan. And besides, she owes us 100 bucks for our recovery mission.

Another thing, Captain, while I have your attention, do you think Lucinda is sharp enough to pick up on the lead about the car now being repaired and the ring found during the repair and the fact that the smell coming from the closed up car that day when she first saw it at the ranch will now give rise to the fact that the smell could be from the deposit of dried blood, and could that blood have come from the late departed Mr. Ted Long? Do you really think that little Mexican girl from Van Horn, Texas, can process all that data?"

"Give it a little time, M#2," I said. "If she needs more data to make a connection, we'll find a way for this little Texas Detective to find her way to unscramble the puzzle."

After a few days at the ranch just playing cowboy and checking the heifers with the Field boys, I decided it was time to make an appearance one more time at The Furniture Mart and deliver the class ring to Samantha, since she is the one who requested we check out the old Red Sedan in the first place.

Hello, Samantha

As I was headed out from the ranch to Angelo this bright Fall morning, I remembered the ring and the proposed meeting with Samantha Morgan to drop off Mr. Ted Long's class ring that had been discovered during the repair of The Red Sedan. I had given much thought to just how this presentation should come off and how I should refrain from getting involved in any conversation or discussion about this matter in general with anyone.

I decided I would just walk in and say, "Samantha, this is the only jewelry that the repairmen reported they found while making repairs to my Red Sedan."

As I arrived at the front of The Furniture Mart, I noticed that there was only one car parked out front in the office staff's parking spots, and that car was not the fancy BMW that Samantha had traded for in Austin several months ago.

I opened the front door and was not too surprised to see that Cherry Longwell was now the only good looking gal sitting behind the big office desk. I knew where Lucinda was now residing, but I still didn't know what she was up to, even if the answers were tucked away right here in this big warehouse Furniture Mart.

"Hi, Cherry. Where is your partner, Samantha? I have that ring you got so upset about at the ranch the other day and I think I should give it to Samantha, since she is the one that caused me to spend 100 bucks in hopes her diamond necklace would turn up as the workmen repaired my car."

"She's not here, Cowboy, as you can plainly see, and I don't give a damn if I ever see that Blonde Bitch again. Fact is when I got back from the ranch the other day, I confronted her about the ring and the disappearance of my sister's brother-inlaw Ted Long. Seems she didn't know or want to talk about Mr. Ted Long or even say if she knew him, or what the hell his class ring was doing in her Red Sedan. She was lying. I know it for sure. You get to know someone after you have been a close friend and a business associate for over four years. Yes, she was damn sure lying and so she just up and takes off and that was four days ago. I've contacted our company attorney and asked him to draw up the papers so I can get out of this business while there is still something left to sell. I just don't want to be anywhere around her and if that means taking a loss to get out, then so be it."

I left the ring on the big desk and said my goodbyes to Cherry Longwell, who by this time had worked herself up tight, no doubt because of all the stress of her finding out that her great friendship with Samantha Morgan had gone down the tubes in such a short time.

As I got into my pickup, I was confronted with two very pressing questions that would have to come to a head sooner or later. One question for sure was why was Lucinda Morales so concerned about what seemed to be centered around the ownership of The Furniture Mart and the two nice looking gals that used to own and operate it as partners.

The second question that was no doubt on a lot of people's minds was, just where in the hell was Samantha Morgan, who could become the most important person of interest when all this came into better focus as to what had been going on here in Angelo at The Furniture Mart and what did she have to do with the disappearance of Mr. Ted Long?

M#2 started on me, as to just why in the hell were we getting deeper in this mess, rather than drawing away from it, as we had discussed.

MEANWHILE BACK AT THE RANCH

After all the diversions, I found it pure joy just getting back into the routine of working on the ranch. I met with the Field boys and we worked the heifers that were doing just fine on the Dove Creek Ranch.

M#2 and I spent several days working on fences and just picking up junk that had been left by the previous ranch owner. This timeout period gave us time to go over all the facts that had taken place since I had acquired the Dove Creek Ranch, and, brother, there were plenty.

One evening as I was just sitting out back on the Patio having myself a cool Rum and Coke, the phone rang and that sweet, little voice of Lucinda Morales jarred me awake when she said, "Could we come over to the Dove Creek Ranch and have a visit with you about needing to clear up some very unusual events that seem to be centered around The Junction on County Road CC-26 and your ownership in the Dove Creek Ranch?"

My answer right quick was, "Sure, Lucinda. You're always welcome over here at the ranch. But just who in the hell is 'we' and what is it you want from me?"

Her reply was, "Thanks, Ron. Inspector Carlos Ortega and Deputy Bill Simmons of the Crime Division of the Texas Department of Texas Rangers will be coming with me. See you tomorrow after lunch. Love ya, Cowboy."

M#2 exclaimed in what seemed to be a rather calm voice, "Well, Big Boy, you sure did get the sweet, little

Mexican gal from Van Horn back in the loop and it looks like she's bringing enough help to string you up with the same rope."

I took a deep breath and decided I should finish my Rum and Coke before I could start thinking about the visit from the Texas Department of Public Safety and the long arm of the Texas Rangers.

For sure, right after lunch, two Texas Highway Patrol Cars pulled up in front of the ranch house. After a brief introduction by Lucinda, I shook hands with both Inspector Ortega and Deputy Simmons and before M#2 could say anything, I made note of the fact that all three officers were armed.

First thing out of the box was that Lucinda turned to me and asked if I would go over the facts I talked to her about in my visit with her in Austin concerning the strange happenings at the area referred to as The Junction or as the kids referred to as The Hide Out.

I started from the beginning about how I had first noticed soon after I had purchased the ranch that my fence was cut with a big hole from ground level to the second barb-wire and that lots of apparently human traffic of sorts seemed to be coming and going down to a dirt tank just inside my property line, somewhat below the parking area of where the two dumpsters are located. I went on to say that every time I fixed the fence, by the next time I came by this location, the fence would be cut again and whatever was going on was still in full swing. I then made a point to the two male officers that I had taken Lucinda over by this same spot one day when we were just touring the ranch.

I told all present about contacting the Sheriff and that he informed me this was a long established place for teens to meet and drink beer, possibly smoke some pot and no doubt have a roll in the grass. Aside from his statements, he did nothing about these happenings over to Dove Creek Ranch.

On one of my visits to this area I noticed that the area around the dumpsters, after a little shower, showed signs of heavy foot traffic and it looked like something might have been dragged over to one of the dumpsters.

Other than that, there was nothing else to cause me any more concern, other than the fact that I was getting damn tired of having to come over and fix the pasture fence. That's when I put up the "No Trespassing" notice and also the fact that I would prosecute all violators.

Then I made a point to Lucinda and her group that I went over to the County Landfill Field Office and met with the supervisor and the two drivers that work the part of the county that takes in the Dove Creek Ranch area. Both men had seen my sign at The Junction location dumpsters but had no information about anything unusual being associated with their weekly pickup from this site.

Mr. Sandoval, the head driver, did make note of the fact that one time earlier this Fall one of his dumpsters failed to pass the sanitation inspection required by the County Environmental Officer due to some form of liquid substance that had dried and they were unable to remove the crusted matter from the bottom of one of the dumpsters; that is, until they steamcleaned it several times.

The law group seemed to be waiting for me to ask them to sit down and have a cup of coffee so they could hear more about my ownership of the Dove Creek Ranch.

M#2 cautioned me to hold up on discussing anything about the Red Sedan, unless they brought it up. He seemed to think they were here for another reason altogether.

I felt like I should let Lucida know just how I felt about her setting me up, and that good Marines don't like girlfriends to use them as spearheads, especially in what might be a criminal investigation.

So everyone sat down and I started a pot of coffee. Before they could asked another question about the Dove Creek Ranch, I just came right out and directed my statements at Lucinda. "Lucinda, you came to this ranch under false pretenses from the very beginning and from the beginning you have shown too much interest in The Junction area. When you left the ranch that morning, you went right back up to the dumpster site and walked all around the area. You must have been there some time, because your muddy footprints were all over the place. I followed your car tracks, as they turned left to The Junction area when you left out of the gate and, as we all know, that's not the road back to El Dorado. So what the hell is going on with you people and just why in the hell have you picked me to fill in the blanks."

No one spoke up and I felt sure I wasn't going to hear their reason for investigating this area of the County. Inspector Ortega spoke up and mentioned the fact that I was not the main part of their interest in whatever they were doing over in this area of Irion County, but he failed to say Dove Creek Ranch wasn't.

However, he did have just one more question for me. "Captain Heard, I'd like to know just where you got all this money to buy this ranch?"

M#2 quickly whispered in my left ear, "Don't tell the bastard anything. He already must have checked us out, after you pumped a big story in Lucinda when she asked you just how you came to own the Dove Creek Ranch. He's just for sure trying to get some more statements from us."

My quick response was, "Inspector Ortega, that is none of your damn business and so I guess this official business by the Texas Law Department is over." Lucinda never even gave me a look, as she and her group headed for the door.

M#2 hollered right out, "Don't leave mad, fellows, the coffee is almost ready."

I then sat down for a good cup of ranch coffee and decided it was about time to try and put this mystery of The Junction site into some sort of focus.

THE COUNT DOWN

After Lucinda and her fellow Texas Officers left, I decided it was time to get all the facts down and in some sort of order, as to just what this cowboy had got involved in so that M#2 and I could see just where we had been and just how we needed to handle our involvement.

One fact was the murder of Ted Long by the Black Widow Samantha Morgan, and another was just what was Lucinda's interest in the Dove Creek Ranch and how this unknown tied in with The Angelo Furniture Mart and, more specifically, Samantha's and Cherry's past ownership of that business.

M#2, without a request from me, jumped right into the fire and said, "First things first, Captain Cowboy Heard. It seems to me you've been getting a little tender around the eyes when you think of Mr. Ted Long's family not knowing just where he went and if he's ever coming home. I kind of agree it would be best to let them know where they can find him, but just how in the hell are you going to get the word out without getting us into more trouble than we can ever handle?"

Without much concern whether M#2 understood or not, I simply said, "Samantha Morgan will just have to tell the authorities what happened and where they can find the man who tried to rape her and got shot three times before he got the message of just what 'No' means."

M#2's response was, "Great news, Captain. Just how in the hell do you propose to get that little chore done?"

"It will come to me, M#2. Don't get all in a sweat. Have I ever left you out in the cold without an answer before?"

I spent most of the rest of the afternoon just going over all the matters that seemed to be bothering M#2 at this time, but I didn't come up with any thing or any way to bring all the mess to a conclusion.

After several hours of unproductive thought, I finally decided the best method to bring up the two most important matters that seemed to involve the ranch and me would be to start over again with Lucinda and see if she could be spoon-fed just a few more details, in hopes she would start to trust me enough to perhaps pass on a little info about whatever had caused her to concentrate so much on The Junction area.

M#2 was much more in step with this type of spy work. He came right out and suggested we consider the anonymous phone call routine; you know, where someone calls in and leaves no name but does give up some very pertinent information about what he might have heard while drinking beer one night at the local watering hole.

THE DAY OF RECKONING

That very afternoon, John Field, the younger of the Field brothers, who had just come in from checking the family heifers, knocked on the front door and said that he needed to have a little visit with me and asked if he could come in for a spell?

My response was, "Sure, John, come on in and have a cup of good ranch coffee."

He came right to the point and inquired about the State Highway Patrol cars that he had seen leaving the ranch earlier this same afternoon. I had nothing to hide, so I told him about Lucinda and the two other officers that had come over to the Dove Creek Ranch to ask some questions of me. For instance, did I know anything about some of the goings on around this part of the County, mainly, The Junction area?

Then I went over the facts that I had been confronted with, from when I first purchased the ranch and it all started with the hole in the fence and the foot traffic down to the surface tank in pasture #2. I even threw in the bit about my reporting my findings to the Sheriff and then going as far as talking to the two dumpster pick-up drivers that worked this area. So I reported I found out nothing and therefore was unable to help them out with whatever they seem to be investigating in and around the Dove Creek Ranch.

John took a deep breath and said, "Ron, I have something to report to you that just might have some bearing on what could be causing those police folks to be so tight mouthed about what's been going on around this location in Irion County."

He then suggested we take a drive over to the lower part of pasture #2 so he could show me what he discovered the other day, while looking for some of their heifers that had been grazing in that area. Before I could even get my hat on, M#2 recounted the Marine Corps safety creed, "Recognize the enemy and always play it cool. If you need to kill, shoot first and move on."

"The problem as I see it, Captain Heard, is that you may not be able to shoot as many people as you need to, if this mystery keeps on growing."

I let John drive so he could find whatever he wanted to talk to me about and it wasn't any time until we arrived at a location just a few hundred yards east of the surface tank in pasture #2. We got out and walked over to the tank and he suggested we sit down on an old log so he could explain to me just why we were here and what else he was about to show me.

M#2 said, "We are all ears, Cowboy John, so let's get on with it." John took another one of his deep breaths and said, "Ron, this area and further deep down the hill through them bushes over there is what in these parts is known as a Hemp Weed Camp. This camp location is a place where all kinds of folks, far and wide, come to smoke hemp weed or should I say, marijuana, so as to reach the more understanding qualities of The Greater Open Mind."

He went on to explain, "The original Hemp Weed Camp People started hundreds of years ago way down in South America, no doubt with the Aztec tribes, and as the cult worked its way up through Mexico over the next 100 years, they went into Texas. I hear they ran out of Hemp Weed and took to smoking pure marijuana. I called them a cult, because you had to swear and pledge part of your wellbeing to the cause of The Greater Open Mind. I guess you could say, if you joined up with the group, you had better do as you're told or something horrible might happen to you and your family.

I come to know some of these people my last year in high school over to El Dorado High. I think was about three years ago. At first it seemed like something I might like to try and so I kind of let them think I just might like to join up with them.

But it wasn't long till I just couldn't go no further with their kind of directions, when they asked me to cut out a few of my Pop's good mares and see that they ended up over to the Hatley Brothers Ranch down by The Junction so they could be hauled on down to Mexico as a trade for a batch of pure marijuana. I just couldn't steal from my own family for the habit of so many worthless Hemp Weed Smoking People who I hadn't even met.

I told my contact that I was not suited for this type of life and so I didn't want to join up with folks that required me to steal from my family. About a week after I made my choice not to be with the Hemp Weed Smokers, Sheriff Thompson, from over to El Dorado, stopped me in my pickup this side of town one day and more or less gave me a good scare. It seems he's not just one of the regulars. He's the Kingpin of the Hemp Weed Smokers for this whole damn territory.

He said, in just so many words, that if I wanted to grow old in Irion County, Texas, and enjoy my family, I'd better forget about ever being contacted about this little social club of country folks who get together now and then for fun and recreation. And so to make sure I understood what he had said, he up and hit me right in the stomach.

As I lay there on the ground trying to get my breath, which is still hard to come by at times, he put his big foot right on my head and ground my face in the gravel and said, "John. did you understand what I just told you about my friends and their doings?"

I managed to say, 'Yes, I understood every word you said.' He kicked me in the ribs and left me lying right there on the road.

Ron, I know you are wondering why I'm here telling you all this stuff, but you need to know who your enemies are, because I think with the buying of this ranch you have already caused the Hemp Weed Smokers to move on out of this area and locate somewhere else. It just could be that some of those folks might take a notion to maybe make your life a little more complicated than what you might have planned on. I do believe you are not the type of fellow to run scared and if push comes to shove, I want to be on your side to get even with the Sheriff who needs a coming down."

I sat there in a state of wonderment, I guess I was waiting for M#2 to respond and here it came, "Captain, it's time to lock and load and I suggest we get our weapons out and give them a good cleaning, so we don't have any misfires when the enemy comes looking for us or we go looking for them."

After I gave myself a few minutes to digest the information John had just unloaded on me, I said, "Well, John, just what else was there you wanted to show me about his area that you are now calling 'a Hemp Weed Smokers Camp'."

He took off walking south from the tank and gave me a hand signal to follow him, as he pushed on through the heavy brush while following a very faint trail. In about five minutes or so we arrived at a small clearing with a cluster of large cedar trees rimming the area, as if they had been planted for some sort of protection from the rest of the surrounding area.

Right in the center of this walled cedar tree complex was a very strange looking mud hut standing about four foot high and being almost 30 or so feet long with only one entrance and that was in the front. The structure appeared to be only six to eight feet wide and there were no windows on either side.

M#2 said, "Would you look at that Mexican house. These folks must have been little people who must have loved to crowd in on top of each other and enjoy close in company."

John turned around and faced me and said. "Captain, this is a Hemp Weed Smokers' gathering place. When the group is called for a gathering, they all show up here at a given time and move into the Camp Hut. Sometimes as many as thirty people crowd in and sit on the floor cross legged and after a few speeches or chants, pure marijuana is passed out to all present and a simultaneous light up is called for by the leader. Due to the design of the camp hut very little puffs of marijuana smoke ever get to leave the interior of the smoke hut. So now everyone present gets a 100% chance of exercising the true meaning of The Greater Open Mind."

"Damn, John, it seems to me this bunch of folks is just plain dumbstruck over the need to smoke marijuana and do this open minded thing, whatever that is."

"That's about it, Captain. But you need to understand these people can get plumb crazy after one of these meetings and you damn sure don't want to be around when they stop smoking and singing.

As you can tell, this smoke hut has not been used in some time and I figure it's because you went to the Sheriff and the County Sanitation people with your complaint about what you thought were kids trespassing on your property. Just about that time, your law officer girlfriend shows up in these parts and begins to ask too many questions about just what might be going on in and around The Junction area. I hear the Sheriff has moved the camp west of here toward the Sonora area."

John went on to say, "It would be best if you don't try to intercede with these people in any way, until you know what all your options are and just how strong your outside help is going to be. And further more, pull in your horns and stop being so casual and talkative with the locals over to El Dorado, because you could be talking to one of the Hemp Weed Smokers."

John and I drove on back to the ranch headquarters and John said his goodbyes in a very serious tone, as he headed down the road to his own ranch.

That left me sitting cold turkey in the pickup, just waiting for M#2 to start his assessment and analysis of the Hemp Weed Smokers, who must have staked out their site long before Tom Tyler decided to sell his ranch to me. And just maybe he was a Hemp Weed Smoker. I stopped M#2 right there and reminded him that if that were the case, Old Tommy Foster would have told us about it, because he had worked here on this very ranch on and off for 10 years prior to the sale.

I noticed it was passed time for a good ranch mixed Rum and Coke, so I headed for the house and a quiet period, so as to reorganize my thinking and get a hold on just what was happening or, should I say, already had happened to the new owner of The Dove Creek Ranch.

Nothing But The Facts

No doubt Lucinda's asking all the questions around these parts had sent a strong message to the Cult that perhaps the long arm of the law was closing in on their social club and the manner in which they explored The Greater Open Human Mind. I was ready to bet that when they found out that this very day several officers from the Texas Department of Public Safety paid a call on the Dove Creek Ranch action, it would no doubt send some chills up and down their brain stems and just might short out their reasoning of The Greater Open Mind.

After I finished my first Rum and Coke, I came up with the reasoning to make sure Lucinda didn't cool off on her efforts to discover the real purpose of her investigation of The Junction Area. Taking into consideration the idea that M#2 had come up with, I decided I would call Lucinda anonymously and suggest that she might just find what she was looking for, if more notice was given to Sheriff Thompson's actions. He might reveal some hard facts for her to consider. However, don't trust him, for he could be dangerous.

That seemed like a great idea to start the ball rolling. The only question remaining was how was I going to do this without bringing the forces of The Texas Rangers down on The Dove Creek Ranch.

I spent the next few days just working around the ranch, wondering what event would surface next, when I came up with the idea to drive over to Spring Creek and make the call to Lucinda's home answering service and leave her the mystery message. I decided it would be best to let M#2 do the calling. He had a voice no one around these parts had ever heard.

On Saturday when I got back from Spring Creek at about sundown, I noticed that the main gate to the ranch was wide open. As I approached the headquarters I was surprised to see Samantha Morgan's black BMW parked right in front of the ranch house. Samantha was asleep or passed out in the back seat. She looked like a worn rag doll which had been left out in the rain overnight. Her appearance was way off base for the once good-looking 35 year old woman.

I got out of my pickup and started for the car, when right on key, M#2 said, "Cowboy, ain't that there woman the Dove Creek Black Widow? Don't you remember what a good shot she used to be, and still could be?"

My response was quick, "You're right, Marine."

So I hollered out, "Samantha, is that you curled up in the backseat of your car?" As if she was just resting and waiting for me to make my appearance, Samantha Morgan, the now located mystery gal, rose up ever so slowly from her nest and said, "Ron, I sure need to talk with you about this ring." She was tightly holding the little plastic sack which contained her late lover's ring, which I knew was now crying out for acknowledgement.

I moved over to the car and opened the door to help her out, as I had already noticed she was ruffled and her clothes were dirty. I do believe she must have been wearing them for days. There was some luggage on the floor next to her, so I latched hold of one of the bags and with my free hand helped her to her feet, as we started for the house.

She seemed to be very weak, so I suggested we sit in the kitchen; I would fix us a sandwich and perhaps a cup of coffee or maybe even a good stiff drink. She said very little as I was preparing the food. Her only comment was, "I just can't seem to get things straight anymore, and I'm so confused over your finding this ring in my old Red Sedan."

I didn't feel like it was the time to get any conversation going about Samantha's past or present actions, until I could get her lined out on just what I wanted to talk to her about. For damn sure, rambling through her mixed thoughts might not accomplish anything worthwhile to the real problem both she and I knew would have to surface sooner or later.

I grabbed her bag and motioned for her to follow me to the spare bedroom and suggested she might want to freshen up a little, since we have plenty of time to talk about whatever she wanted and time out here on the ranch is plentiful.

I opened the door to the bathroom and turned on the water to the bathtub, hoping she might take the hint that a good hot bath might make her feel somewhat better. I hoped she would follow my lead, and I said, "I'll be out in the den whenever you're ready for this talk."

After about 45 minutes or so when she hadn't appeared, I ventured back to the spare bedroom, only to find Samantha Morgan had turned back the covers on the big double bed and was now sound asleep in some of the very furniture she and her crew had sold me back when this strange contact between the Marine and Dove Creek Black Widow began.

M#2, who had remained silent up to this point, blurted out, "Captain, you sure can draw a lot of flies with the least amount of sugar. Just what in the hell do you think is the most important conversation you want or need to discuss with the now sleeping beauty?"

I tried to whiff him off, but he kept coming on strong about just what I shouldn't be discussing with Samantha under any type of her persuasions. It was finally decided that there would be no admitting to anything about The Junction matter. Further more, I promised I would not give up the diamond necklace that was still hanging in the shower, no matter how touched my heart strings were, even when all the tears started flowing. The rhythm of her story would be based on her interpretation of the events up to now, should she want to bring them into our discussion.

By this time it was almost 5:30 pm. The evening shadows were starting to close on the ranch on this cool Fall day. My house guest continued to sleep off the events of several days of, should I say, "Being on the run."

Once again I checked on her and she was still dead to the world. I decided that this important meeting between the Marine Cowboy and the once Queen of The Furniture Mart, if it could survive the night, would just have to take place tomorrow when our guest was well rested and back more or less to her old confident self.

I spent the rest of the evening listening to the radio and treating myself to several homemade Rum and Cokes, just so my mind might be rested and fresh for whatever was coming down the pike tomorrow.

Needless to say, it was a restless night and once again M#2 awakened me at intervals to see if the Marine Issued 45 I had borrowed from the Corps was cocked and ready and waiting. It was always under my pillow, just in the event the Dove Creek Black Widow came a'calling for something other than the mating period.

I was up early drinking my second cup of coffee when I heard a slight noise.

So I turned slightly to the left as Miss Samantha Morgan ventured down the hallway and made her beautiful entrance toward the kitchen. She was still clad in her white cotton kind of see-through shirt-length nightshirt. No need to get tangled up in thoughts and dreams. This was a great looking woman and in a heartbeat I almost forgot about all the past action that Saturday morning not too long ago, as I lay deep in the bush and became a witness to the shooting of the late Ted Long, which I did nothing about.

And now, so to speak, the aftermath may have come home to roost. Samantha glided up to the table and so gracefully slid in the chair next to me without the least bit of concern that her appearance could cause my distraction for anything we might have to talk about.

Her first words were, "Coffee, please. Make it black. Do you have some sort of robe I might borrow? It's just a little cool this early in the morning."

M#2 clamored out without any reservations, "Captain, she don't need no robe. I personally don't think it's cool in here. Fact is, I seem to be sweating just a bit."

I stood up and moved over to the sink and poured my guest a fresh cup of hot ranch coffee and then headed off to my room up front to see if I still had my old Marine Corps issued hospital robe.

As I headed back to the kitchen, robe in hand, Samantha was standing in the filtered morning sunlight that had just now found its way into the ranch kitchen. I took a deep breath, as she extended her arms out for me to engage her beautiful looking body in this old worn out robe that was starting to look much better the closer I got.

We both sat down and tried to drink our coffee, when she said, "Ron, thanks for the use of the room and the hot bath. I was in need of some creature comforts and you must have known it. It's been a rough 10 days or so since I had the confrontation with Cherry over this damn ring and I just haven't been able to get my thoughts together, due to several pressing matters I can't seem to shake off.

Could I ask you a few questions that keep surfacing every time I think of this damn ring? You said it was found in the Red Sedan by the auto body workers over to Odessa?"

M#2 whispers, "Here it comes, Captain. This is called hook and bait and you are the prey."

"It's nice to see you, Samantha, and I'm sorry to see you so disturbed and more so to hear that you and Cherry have had a falling out and are now thinking of selling out of the furniture business."

Samantha responded in such a quick, high pitched voice, "Who said I'm selling out of the furniture business?"

It kind of caught me offbase, so I told her that when I delivered the ring to The Furniture Mart, Cherry was the only one around, She said she had a confrontation with you over the ring ownership, because the inscription indicated the ring belonged to her brother-in-law, a fellow named Ted Long, who had been missing for almost a month. She felt like you knew something about his disappearance, since his ring, after all, had been found in your old Red Sedan.

No doubt this last statement blew the lid off the calmness of what had first seemed like a very exciting day for this West Texas Cowboy. Samantha was now staring daggers through me, or maybe it was Cherry.

After a rather long period of silence, Samantha still with her high pitched voice exclaimed, "That's Bull Shit. That marijuana smoking bitch can't sell that business under any condition. It was my money that put the deal together in the first place. All she had was a few contacts that will no doubt end up getting us both in deep trouble with the long arm of the law. For your information, Cherry and I were casual friends at best, when I asked her if she would like to go in with me and open a design and furniture business right here in Angelo.

She had very little capital to put into the would-be operation, but she did indicate she had some great contacts that would get us some up front money fast. So that's how 'The Angelo Furniture Mart' got started. Several weeks after the doors were open for business, Cherry said she had developed some good leads with Mexican furniture dealers that wanted an outlet for the

Mexican furniture trade here in West Texas. All we had to do was just warehouse loads of their furniture and then some other contact would call us for a pickup date. We would get paid for handling and storage."

Samantha was now settling down a little, but she continued to go on about her past and present relationship with Cherry and the business deal they had struck.

"Well, it wasn't ten days before a small truck showed up at our loading dock with what turned out to be our first load of Mexican furniture. The load received was only about eight or so large pieces of wood furniture. The items were stored in one of the back rooms and nothing more was said. I found out later that there was no bill or invoice or any kind of paper work attached to this load of furniture.

One morning about a week later, I was informed by one of our warehouse workers that the Mexican furniture had been picked up and this envelope was left with Cherry's name on it. When Cherry showed up, I handed her the envelope. She opened it and produced five one-hundred dollar bills as payment for the storage."

I was getting a little restless. Our conversation didn't seem to be getting us anywhere, at least not to the issues at hand, a discussion about the lost ring that had belonged to Ted Long. So I asked Samantha why she had referred to Cherry as "a marijuana smoking bitch" in her previous outburst.

Samantha hesitated for a few seconds and then said, "The Mexican furniture deal turned out to be just a way for the marijuana growers in Mexico to smuggle their product into West Texas by having it hidden away in the confines of the wooden furniture."

The problem was that Cherry had always been a marijuana smoker and once she found where the contraband was hidden, she began to help herself to the stash. This trade between the Mexicans and us went on for over a year. We were always paid in cash. The problem was that it didn't take the contact people long to figure out that someone was breaking into their goods and they were being shorted on their delivery. It pointed right back to us at The Furniture Mart.

One afternoon just before closing time, two very tough looking cowboy type men showed up and asked to talk with Cherry Longwell. She wasn't in, so I asked the two men if there was something I could do for them.

I was told in a brief statement that someone connected with this business had been breaking into their goods and helping themselves to what turned out to be marijuana of the highest quality. One of the men then handed me a statement charging The Furniture Mart with $5,000.00 for goods received. Samantha went on to say, "So now you know how all this trouble got started and, yes, it was due to Cherry's marijuana habit."

M#2, without being called on, spoke right up and said, "I guess we now know where the Hemp Weed Smokers were getting their so called 100% pure smoking material from. So now, Captain, what do you think our next move ought to be?"

After all this factual one-sided news from Samantha began to taper off, I thought it was about time that I brought her into the big picture, which would describe to her a friend she might have thought she had by the name of Lucinda Morales, an Undercover Narcotics Officer with the Texas Department of Public Safety.

I then told Samantha what I knew about Lucinda and her undercover work and that I believed she was onto the marijuana trail that she and Cherry were providing for the Hemp Weed Smokers of Irion County. And, by the way, one of the officials of the Hemp Weed Smokers was the Head Sheriff of Irion County and his office was in El Dorado.

I continued with the story and told Samantha that just a few days ago, Lucinda and two other State Police Officers were here at the ranch asking questions about all the goings on around these parts and, more so, at The Junction. Samantha then asked me in a very low toned voice, "Did you tell her about the ring you say you found in my old Red Sedan?"

"No, I didn't. Fact is the issue about the Red Sedan never came up, and, yes, the workers did find that ring in the car when they were repairing it."

Just then M#2 whispered in my ear, "Tell the Black Widow she still owes us $100.00, even if you are lying to her about the Red Car and the ring."

There was little or no response coming from either of us, after I finished my little episode. The silence that followed was making M#2 nervous, when Samantha spoke up as she leaned across the kitchen table toward me, no doubt to get my close up attention. Her statement was right to the point. "Ron Heard or Captain or whatever you want to be called, you are a liar. You know more about my problems than you are telling."

Samantha then stood up, took off the robe and threw it on the table. "I won't be needing this any more. I'm packing my things and getting out of here. She turned and headed for the spare bedroom when all of a sudden she stopped, made an abrupt turn around, and walked back to where I was still sitting at the kitchen table.

"Yes, I did shoot Ted Long," she said, "but you already know this. It was self-defense. He had tried to rape me and had already hit me violently several times in the process of this physical rape. When I finally got him off of me and out of the car, I just lost my cool. I walked around the car and before I knew it, I shot him again and again. But you know this because you were right there. I know you were there watching, even though I never saw you.

But since that horrible day, every time I met you, I felt your presence as if you were behind the trees or in the bushes. I even fired a shot out into the pasture where I thought you were hiding. And, yes, I did see your footprints. You left them in the mud from the fence line to the dumpster, while I was gone up the road. Then I returned suddenly, after I learned that my beautiful diamond necklace was not around my neck and it wasn't in the car either. It was my hope I could find it in the mud where the car was parked or perhaps next to the dumpster.

I saved your biggest lie to the last. The fact is that Ted Long was wearing his ring and Rolex watch when with great difficulty, I managed to work him into the dumpster. So not only did you steal from the dead, but you had first hand knowledge of this situation and are now guilty yourself by not turning me in that very morning."

For the first time in all my years of dealing with M#2, he was not to be found in any of my thought patterns.

By this time Samantha had started crying and I was caught without a clear thought or word of defense, as to why I had gotten myself into this kind of mess that could drag me into, no doubt, some of the worst trouble I had ever been in.

I reached out and grabbed her arm and pulled her closer to the table. Then I asked her to sit a moment. I held her and tried to comfort her a little. "Samantha, yes, I was there. It was quite by accident. I was out in the pasture getting ready to fix a hole in the fence, when I first heard you scream at your attacker. I had no idea who it was, but I was coming to your aid when you fired the first shot.

Yes, I was now an accessory to the shooting of Ted Long. I knew it was in self-defense, but after you regained your composure, so to speak, and, ever so quickly, you fired two more shots into what I guessed was the body of Ted Long. It was never my intention to turn you in and that is still my same feeling. Yes, I took the ring and the watch from his dead body and to this day, I still don't know why I did a thing like that. It's way out of my character."

Samantha was now holding onto me, as if I was her long lost friend and she was still sobbing. I hoped with all my feelings that she didn't ask me, "What am I going to do now?" For the first time in my life, I was lost for an answer that could be helpful to someone in such need. And that included me also.

M#2 finally surfaced and said, "You're in so deep now, you might as well 'fess up and go get her diamond necklace. It's still hanging on the right hand faucet in the shower. If I were you, I'd just forget about the hundred bucks she owes us. If things don't change here pretty quick, we might not have any use for money anyway."

So I got up from the table and retrieved the necklace. As I sat back down next to Samantha, I placed the necklace in her hand and said, "Yes, I found it in the mud next to the dumpster."

I thought things to this point were as bad as they could get and couldn't get any worse, but they did. Samantha's sobbing turned into out right crying and shaking. She kept repeating, "It's all over now. It's all over now. There is no place for me to go from this point on. I didn't mean to kill him. I just lost my cool after the beating he had just given me."

I found it next to impossible to control her sobbing. She continued to cry and sob and kept repeating "It's all over for me now."

I put the robe back around her shoulders and began talking to her in hopes she would calm down. Finally she managed to get control of her emotions. She started talking about her divorce from her husband and the fact that at one time she had been so happy and, yes, he had given her this beautiful necklace on their second anniversary.

MOMENT OF TRUTH

In what seemed like an hour, all of a sudden Samantha stood up and again took off the robe and threw it on the table. She blurted out, "It's not your problem. I brought this on myself and I have no one to blame but me. I have no idea why or what your reasons might have been for you to get so involved in my personal life and problems and what possible benefit could this horrible matter be to you. So from here on out, leave me be and stop pushing on me.

As far as I'm concerned, this will be our last discussion and visit. Is that clear and is this simple enough for you to just let me go and forget about that dreadful Saturday morning when all good reasoning went to hell in a hand basket? What ever happens to me from this point forward will be just my concern and my doing."

M#2 said, "Back off, Captain, it ain't going to ever get any better than it is right now. She has just opened the back door for us to exit out of and I suggest we do it in great haste. Whatever else you might have been planning about this entire rotten affair, just cool it and let's get back to cowboying on this good old West Texas Ranch. Speak up! Did you hear me?"

I felt a real uneasiness, or should I say, sadness, as I watched Samantha Morgan drive down the lane to the ranch gate and disappear from view and, I guessed, from The Dove Creek Ranch forever. Her last words kept coming back to me, as I tried to dodge the truth of her meaning, "What possible reason did you have for getting involved in my personal life?"

As I tried to sort out how this conclusion might be a telltale part of my real makeup, M#2 jumped right in the middle of this wonderment and stated, "Just maybe, Captain, you and I aren't used to seeing a pretty white girl shoot her lover over such a trivial matter of romance, or, should I say, a lack of consent."

TIME IS RUNNING OUT

Lucinda called the ranch two days later and again asked permission to come for a short visit. This time she indicated she would come alone. The very next day after her call, which was on a Friday, she showed up at my door around noon with what turned out to be another one of her famous picnic lunches and, no doubt, an appetite for conversation.

We moved out onto the patio, where we had first started this bland affair and after some light conversation, Lucinda came right out and said, "A helicopter flying over The Junction area spotted a mud house structure of sorts, just down from the surface tank in your pasture. You know the area, just below where you reported all the kids were trespassing onto your ranch. Why don't we discuss what you know about this matter, as we take another one of our tours over The Dove Creek Ranch, but head toward that particular area."

So after a quick lunch, off we went in the ranch pickup for an adventure that I knew was going to bring a small part of my problems to a conclusion.

On the way over to pasture #2 I told her how several weeks ago when I was out looking for some of the heifers I was pasturing here on the ranch that I also came across what appeared to be an abandoned mud hut of a most unusual design and construction. Yes, I was concerned about what it was and who built it and what use it was put to and how long it had been abandoned and for what reason.

No doubt it was built during the years Tom Tyler owned this ranch. Were all the kids that had been causing me so much trouble involved in its use and just who was in charge of whatever had been going on inside my fenced ranch pasture?

Before I could say anything more, M#2 started right off by saying, "Don't tell this lady cop anything more than you have to. I do believe she already knows more than you suspect she does."

We arrived at a point in pasture #2 where it was only a short hike through the brush to the small clearing where the mud hut was located. I stayed back a little.

Lucinda walked all around the structure several times, then got down on her hands and knees and shined her flashlight through the small door opening and peered deep into the inside of the large sitting room. She didn't make a full entry, because there were bundles of spider webs hanging and clinging to the mud surface interior that blocked most of her view. That seemed to give her good reason not to investigate any further than she could see from where she was now kneeling.

One thing was for damn sure: this proved that this structure had not been used for some time and even Lucinda agreed with these findings. She got up, dusted herself off as good as possible and then walked over to where I was standing and said, "Ok, Cowboy, what else would you like for The Texas Department of Narcotics to know about just what the hell has been going on around here since you bought this damn ranch."

My reply was swift and to the point, "Get off my back, Lucinda. You have been snooping around here since we first met several months ago and I now for damn sure know that our first meeting was well planned on your part. So don't expect me to fill in the blanks that you are now so concerned with about The Dove Creek Ranch or this damn funny looking mud hut that has now caused you to return to, should I say, my once open arms of hospitality."

Lucinda just stood there a few seconds before she got herself gathered up from my quick, blunt reply and she said, "Can we now just have a truce on all that has happened between us in the past and start fresh right here and now and exchange thoughts that might have a bearing on some very serious assumptions on my part that have to do with gross violations of the Texas Narcotics Laws by someone or even a group of local people in what now appears to be centrally located in the El Dorado and Spring Creek areas?

If your answer is yes, let's head back to house and start with what you know about Samantha Morgan and Cherry Longwell, the owners of The Angelo Furniture Mart, where we all first met. So how about it, Cowboy? Can we get on with this matter? And then I'll fill you in on what we already know."

Remembering what M#2 had already warned me about, I decided to comply with Lucinda's suggestion to a certain extent. However, I would leave her with the questions she would need to research on her own to come to any sort of conclusion about who was involved in her marijuana problems.

The last thing I needed to do was to implicate The Dove Creek Ranch into any question or position that could drag me personally into any future discovery about the matter of Ted Long, should that matter surface, and I was for sure it was going to. I just didn't know how and when.

The most pressing question for me was how I was going to get free of Samantha Morgan and her problems and should I somehow find a way to notify the authorities about the hidden body of Ted Long who is now located in the Irion County Landfill.

THE STORY STARTS TO UNFOLD

After we got back to the house and ventured out to the patio, I started off with guarded comments concerning the fact that I knew nothing about Samantha Morgan and Cherry Longwell and their personal relationship or their business association in The Angelo Furniture Mart, other than what I already knew and had always been involved with and that was her selling me all the furniture for this ranch house.

I said, "I do know for damn sure that you're the one that started the big issue over that wrecked Red Sedan that I bought secondhand from the folks over to El Dorado. Ever since that time, both Cherry and Samantha have been to this ranch individually to discuss several matters other than who owned the damn car and what did it have to do with the disappearance of Cherry Longwell's ex-brother-in-law and his class ring and a missing diamond necklace.

It appears to me that once you as a detective find out what's going on between those two women, you might just have some answers to a lot of your questions. As to the marijuana problems you seem to be so interested in, I hear you can get a sack full of marijuana over to El Dorado by just hanging out at The Watering Hole. But you already know that, because that's where you first started asking all your questions about the local people as far back as several months ago."

M#2 came right on and said, "Great presentation, Captain. That should slow her down and hopefully cause her to get the hell off The Dove Creek Ranch and continue her investigation somewhere else."

Once again, Lucinda gave me another one of her famous "go to hell" looks, that is, just before she turned on her heels and headed for the front door. She did manage to say, "Ok, Cowboy, if that's the way you want to play, then so be it. The Texas Department of Public Safety can handle this matter without your help, but if we find your footprints anywhere along the trail, don't expect any favors from me. You have just given me notice that you don't intend to cooperate with us and this on-going investigation and, for damn sure, this is the last of our so-called friendly picnic meetings we will ever have."

I followed her out to her car and just before she got her car started and headed out the front gate, I leaned inside the driver's side window and kissed her on the cheek. Then I whispered in her ear, "Sweet Thing, be very damn careful when and if you feel you need to take the local Sheriff over to El Dorado into your confidence. I've heard he can be mean to the point he is dangerous, if asked too many questions."

M#2 called to mind that we were just plain cowboys here at The Dove Creek Ranch and now we're on our on. We shouldn't look for any kind of help from anyone around here and should keep our secrets to ourselves from here on out. His last personal comment to me before I closed him out was, "What are we going to do if Samantha changes her mind and decides to involve us in the death of Mr. Ted Long? Just what is our position going to be in this matter, if the long arm of the law comes calling?"

I went back into the house and decided to pour my self a Rum and Coke. I was left with this same haunting question. What can I do if Samantha decides to implicate me in her accidental but deliberate killing of Ted Long? After a few days of just plain ranch life, I decided to drive over to El Dorado and just hang out with the locals at the Williams Sinclair Service Station to see if I could pick up on just anything that might have a bearing on the so-called marijuana investigation in the El Dorado and Spring Creek communities.

Hot Shot the owner and his little brother were not around and, in fact, there wasn't any of the old gang hanging around either. The only person around was one of the garage workers by the name of Felipe. So I got right up in his face and asked him where the patron Mr. Williams was. His answer was that most everyone was over to the Courthouse being talked to by the Texas Rangers and other police people and had been there most of the day.

I got back in my car and made a swing by the Courthouse and, for sure, the entire parking lot was full of police cars. M#2 responded to this sudden show of police power and said, "Let's just get the hell out of here and let the dust settle wherever it's going to. I'm sure they don't need our help."

I went back to the ranch and hoped that no new or old faces turned up at my gate and I felt like I needed to answer some more questions about all the strange things that were happening around these parts.

I guess the old saying is true, "No news is good news in troubled times," because for the next three days or so not a word came down the road about all the police action in El Dorado this past week. So finally I couldn't stand it any longer. I jumped in the pickup and headed for Spring Creek, where I was sure I could get some fresh information about whatever was going on in the County.

The little town site of Spring Creek was all hyped up about all the local citizens of the County that had been arrested and charged with not only using marijuana but distributing it for resale to groups of people who belong to certain smoking clubs.

I went over to the bank to talk with Mr. G.S. McGinnis to see if I could get the lowdown on who was being charged and just what was going to happen to all these people, if the charges were for real and held. The old gentleman was sitting right up front in his office swivel chair, just like he had been doing for the last 40 years or so. His first comment to me was, "Hi there, Captain. Good to see you didn't make the list of marijuana smokers, even though the big smokeout had been taking place on your ranch."

I started off our conversation with how I had found the abandoned mud hut just about the same time the Texas State Police had spotted it from their helicopter and then sent an agent over to the ranch to see what I knew about its location right there in what I refer to as pasture #2.

I guessed I made the cut, because after their visit, which was about a week ago, I hadn't heard a word from them. I did see a whole fleet of Texas State Police cars over to the Courthouse in El Dorado the other day. The talk was that some of the locals were hauled in for some form of questioning.

"You got that right, Captain. Twenty one men and eight women have been indicted for distributing and using marijuana and now it appears a grand jury trial is being put together to hear these charges. You can bet your last dollar the trial won't be around these parts, because there ain't that many folks left to serve on the jury."

Mr. McGinnis then produced a list of the people arrested. There were the names of the two Williams brothers and several other people I had met around town. Right there in big print was the big dog himself, Sheriff Thompson of Irion County.

M#2 once again was quick to remind me that the marijuana issue was of record and the officials had closed down the Hemp Weed Smokers Club House. Now we cowboys over to The Dove Creek Ranch could just go back to checking the heifers and doing whatever ranch work needed doing.

M#2 closed off his remarks with a bone chilling statement. "You know, Captain, all we have to worry about is just what the hell The Dove Creek Black Widow is going to do about her last stand with the late Mr. Ted Long."

The End Is In Sight

The local weekly El Dorado newspaper was packed full of the Hemp Weed Smokers news. All the names of the club members were listed, along with a rather long, detailed story about the history of the club and just what their intended purpose was.

After going over the story, M#2 indicated that it was clear to him what their purpose was: to get high on marijuana and plan when to meet again for the so-called, "Opening of a Greater Mind."

The trial location had been moved to Midland County about 125 miles northwest of El Dorado. The rumor was that everyone would probably just get a good warning and a few years of probation. Sheriff Thompson was forced to resign and moved to somewhere in South Texas. Seems he had developed a lot of hard feelings, due to the procedures and hard-handed practices in County law enforcement.

Lucinda called several days after the newspaper stories were printed and was downright friendly about the published facts. She gladly informed me that my footprints had not been found in any of the investigation details that had been uncovered. She went on to say that there would be charges filed against both Samantha Morgan and Cherry Longwell this coming week, based on the indication that they were involved in the distribution of marijuana.

M#2 said, "Well, at least the charge is not going to include the selling of marijuana."

Lucinda asked me if I had heard from Samantha since she last visited The Dove Creek Ranch. It seems they had not been able to locate her to serve the official charge.

I responded, saying that I had not heard from her, nor did I know where she was going when she had left the ranch.

I continued to play cowboy, as to looking after the heifers with John Fields. I always seemed to find something that needed to be repaired or just plain rebuilt, such as barn doors, gates and miles and miles of fence repair.

M#2 mentioned that it looked to him like this was going to be a never ending job.

I decided that it was about time I showed up at the service station in El Dorado, so that all the survivors wouldn't blame me for the law enforcement troubles that had caved in on them over their smoking marijuana and the mud hut located on The Dove Creek Ranch.

In order to have a conversation piece to help break the chill that I felt was now causing concern to all the once dedicated Hemp Weed Smokers, I drove the newly repaired Red Sedan over to El Dorado and parked it right in front of Hot Shot's station. Everyone could see what a $10,000.00 repair job looks like.

No one showed any interest, except Charlie, the one I had purchased the car from in the first place. He came over to the car and gave it a once over and stated, "It appears if you have enough money, you can get almost anything done that needs doing."

He then went on to ask me if this was the same car that had once belonged to that furniture gal by the name of Samantha Morgan? Before I could answer, he went on to say that she and her partner were both being charged for distributing marijuana out of their furniture store in Angelo.

What old Charlie failed to say was it was his group of smokers that were the ones who had received all the marijuana that came by way of The Furniture Mart. We stood around just chewing the fat about all the action that had been going on. It was obvious to me that he had been interviewed by Lucinda Morales, because he just knew too many details about me, the car and all the ongoing police action.

Just as I was ready to leave, Hot Shot Williams, the service station owner and also a charged Hemp Weed Smoker, came over to the car to report that the new sheriff had just called him to indicate that the Texas Department of Public Safety had located a black BMW Sports Sedan registered in the name of Samantha Morgan. It was found parked at the Houston Ship Terminal with a note saying that the body of Ted Long could be located in the Irion

County Landfill with a burial date somewhere around September 17, 1976.

It appeared whoever this Samantha Morgan was, she must of caught a boat ride to nobody knows where.

After this soul crushing bit of news ricocheted through my brain several times, I just decided I better go on back to the ranch to see if I could make any sense to all of what had happened to me over these last several months.

I shook hands with both Hot Shot and Charlie and wished them well in their upcoming trip to Midland. I took a deep seat in the still famous Red Sedan and headed for the ranch.

M#2 in a very determined voice spoke with deep convictions, "Here we are riding home in The Murder Car where The Dove Creek Black Widow silenced her mate's affections. For all we know, she is the very same person who holds our cowboy careers in the palm of her hand and now has taken a boat ride to who knows where . . . AND STILL NO CRY FOR HELP."

www.ingramcontent.com/pod-product-compliance
Lightning Source LLC
Chambersburg PA
CBHW051423280526
45785CB00003B/1143